All the Cool Girls Get Fired

All the Cool Girls Get Fired

How to Let Go of Being Let Go and Come Back on Top

Laura Brown and Kristina O'Neill

EBURY EDGE

UK | USA | Canada | Ireland | Australia
India | New Zealand | South Africa

Ebury Edge is part of the Penguin Random House group of companies
whose addresses can be found at global.penguinrandomhouse.com

Penguin Random House UK
One Embassy Gardens, 8 Viaduct Gardens, London SW11 7BW

penguin.co.uk
global.penguinrandomhouse.com

Penguin Random House UK

First published in the United States by Gallery Books in 2025
This edition published in the United Kingdom by Ebury Edge in 2025

1

Copyright © Laura Brown and Kristina O'Neill 2025
Interior design by Karla Schweer
Jacket design by Magnus Berger
The moral right of the author has been asserted.

Penguin Random House values and supports copyright. Copyright fuels creativity, encourages diverse voices, promotes freedom of expression and supports a vibrant culture. Thank you for purchasing an authorised edition of this book and for respecting intellectual property laws by not reproducing, scanning or distributing any part of it by any means without permission. You are supporting authors and enabling Penguin Random House to continue to publish books for everyone. No part of this book may be used or reproduced in any manner for the purpose of training artificial intelligence technologies or systems. In accordance with Article 4(3) of the DSM Directive 2019/790, Penguin Random House expressly reserves this work from the text and data mining exception.

Printed and bound in Great Britain by Clays Ltd, Elcograf S.p.A.

The authorised representative in the EEA is Penguin Random House Ireland,
Morrison Chambers, 32 Nassau Street, Dublin D02 YH68

A CIP catalogue record for this book is available from the British Library

ISBN 9781529147025

Penguin Random House is committed to a sustainable future
for our business, our readers and our planet. This book is made
from Forest Stewardship Council® certified paper.

MIX
Paper | Supporting
responsible forestry
FSC® C018179

*To all the girls, everywhere.
No one works harder than you.*

Contents

Introduction ... 1

1 / Your Money ... 25

2 / *Lisa Kudrow* ... 47

3 / Do You Need a Lawyer? ... 59

4 / *Tracy Sherrod* ... 77

5 / *Katie Couric* ... 83

6 / Health Care ... 91

7 / *Jennifer O'Connell & Rebecca Quinn* ... 105

8 / *Sallie Krawcheck* ... 113

9 / Mental Health ... 121

10 /	*Tarana Burke*	137
11 /	*Jamie Lee Curtis*	145
12 /	Managing Your Exit and Networking	153
13 /	*Dominique Browning*	167
14 /	*Mika Brzezinski*	175
15 /	Getting Hired	183
16 /	*Lindsay Colas*	195
17 /	Redefine Yourself in the Workplace	201
18 /	*Carol Burnett*	213
19 /	Screw It, Take a Break	221
20 /	*Angela Missoni & Margherita Maccapani Missoni*	227
21 /	Firing Yourself	237
22 /	*Oprah Winfrey*	247
23 /	Onward!	261
24 /	Cut to ... A Year Since We Started Writing This Book	271

Acknowledgments 275

Introduction

So, you got fired—laid off, let go, reduced, restructured, canned, shit-canned. Or if you want to spin it (and we don't suggest you do), you "left." Well, welcome to the party, baby!

The thing is, these days, you probably didn't get fired because you suck at your job. You likely got fired because your industry is changing, morphing, and mutating like one of those AI videos where people have weird hands. The changes are seismic: mind-melting tech advances, company buyouts, changing consumer demand—hey, maybe you just have a crappy boss who doesn't see your value or potential. Tech is laying off tens of thousands of people almost weekly, media is losing its currency, and startups are hitting the wall. Every day there's a different news alert: IBM, Disney, Shell, Apple, Tesla, Mastercard, UPS, geez, even Dyson... the list goes on and on. And, of course, this year thousands of federal employees faced the buzz saw of layoffs wielded by the Trump administration's ostensible Department of Government Efficiency (DOGE). There's no sugarcoating it: it sucks out there right now.

So many people are getting fired, from so many places, there is a TikTok trend of people filming and sharing their layoffs-by-Zoom. We live in a world where getting fired is part of the global discourse, yet few of us women can talk frankly about it, let alone own it. Why? Well, because for generations men have dominated the professional landscape. It has taken us ladies—culturally, politically, personally—so much longer to make our mark, to earn our position (while hard to believe, remember, in the United States, we only earned the right to vote in 1920!). So, when you lose that extremely hard-earned status, it cuts deeper, because it took *so much longer* to achieve it.

That said, though, why should that define you? Why should you *let* it? Remember, you earned a lot of equity during your years grinding it out for your overlords, and you have earned the right to spend it. Everything you've learned, built, and put into practice over your career doesn't just go *poof* when your job goes away. Do not attach your value to where you work; your value lies within *you*. This transition is, in fact, a gateway to a whole new world of opportunity—to leave behind your old obligations and explore what you really love. (Read this in a Brené Brown voice if it helps. It's fine!)

Right this minute, though, you're probably on the couch—by turns pounding out replies to friends' and colleagues' texts, staring at your bank balance permanently open in your browser, wondering what the eff COBRA is, and maybe popping a Xanax.

So, we're here to help. Our goal in writing this book is to acknowledge the shock, confusion, and all the stages of grief that come with losing a job, and pair all of that rough stuff with a pragmatic step-by-step road map to get through this time and emerge stronger. From coping mechanisms and self-care practices to networking strategies and reinvention techniques, *All the Cool Girls Get Fired* is a comprehensive GPS to navigate the path of career recovery and bounce back with more professional mojo than ever.

And while we've both been through it—learning many lessons rapidly during an overwhelming time—we called in the experts. When you are numb from the shock of job loss, we want you to simply open up to any page and learn from the best: how to manage your money, health care, legal representation (should you need it), your mental health, networking, recruiting, leaving a bad job . . . hell, even how and when to take a big ol' break from all of it. And because laws, regulations, and benefits are shifting all the time, we are sharing what you need to know now. Our experts run the gamut from financial columnists to workplace lawyers, healthcare consultants to corporate recruiters. All of them, by the way, are super cool and explain things in English, not abbreviations and acronyms (lady, you're overwhelmed enough). This book contains so much of the information we wished we'd had when we got fired.

Now, of course, we got laid off in the United States. But that special "I lost my job" feeling is the same, wherever you are based, thanks to global consolidation, rampant technological change, the vacillations of the international economy, and a million other things you could never have imagined when you were first hired. You will likely find that your needs (and vulnerabilities) are different, depending on the infrastructure of the country where you live. For example, in the United States, we both immediately freaked out about access to healthcare, but if you live in a country with public healthcare (lucky you!), that might not even make your list. Take some time to seek out comparable support systems in your country to the ones we mention in this book. (Like lawyers, baby. They're everywhere.)

And speaking of getting fired, you know how you think at that moment that it's only happening to you? Well, it isn't. We talked to hugely successful—sometimes, hugely famous—women who, guess what, once got canned, too. And while many of these great ladies seem to "have it all" (hello, Oprah), there were times when they decidedly didn't. We were surprised by how emotional some became when discussing the subject with us, how clear and urgent their memories of losing their jobs were, even if the firing itself was decades ago. Like you, they were panicking about paying the rent or mortgage, had lost their confidence, and were deeply worried about their reputations. But they got up and got on with it, and sometimes fate intervened, helping them not just get back on their feet but to understand their value and want something better for themselves. Their stories are here to not just give you comfort, but to fire up your dreams.

But for now, focus on getting through the day, the week, the month, and onward. And while we know you can't help it, *try* not to overthink all of it. A lot of the trauma of job loss comes from our own irrational decisions.

Once you've digested and owned your firing, you are better

positioned to get your proverbial shit together. To put it simply: we don't want working women to feel this vulnerable again.

Why Should You Listen to Us?

We've spent nearly thirty years in fashion media, an industry obsessed with appearance—surrounded by the slickest of ducks gliding along the pond, praying no one sees their legs paddling furiously underneath (or if they do, at least *notice the shoes, honey*).

And guess what? Both of us got big-time, super publicly fired; two ruffled ducks decanted unceremoniously out of the water. Plop... *et* plop.

But let's go back a bit: From a terrifyingly young age, all we both wanted to do when we grew up was to work at fashion magazines. Now both age fifty (well, technically, Kristina is still gripping tightly to forty-nine), we were teenagers in the early '90s when the world of style was at its shiniest: supermodels were prancing down the runway at Versace shows, the economy was rebounding ferociously from the late '80s crash, and *American Psycho*, well, that was *hilarious*. And maybe best of all, you could get drunk and fall down at a party without anybody filming it. (We both just sighed, audibly.)

The world was grappling with the start of the digital revolution, which was going to reshape our lives in ways we were just starting to understand, while the grunge movement and the rise of hip-hop were challenging the established (and vanilla) notions of fashion and beauty. MTV videos were like runway shows for us suburban kids. On the big screen at the mall, we were glued to cool indies like

Heathers and *Reality Bites*—we would have watched Winona Ryder do her tax returns—and desperately wanted to be Uma Thurman in *Pulp Fiction* (minus the needle of adrenaline to the chest). We were surrounded and nourished by dreamlike images that built people up before, years later, social media started tearing them down.

As a teenager growing up in Australia, Laura was obsessed with those giant, shiny, phone book–sized magazines that magically landed from New York City like Willy Wonka's golden ticket. It was through magazines that she saw not just fashion, celebrity, and glamour, but another world that seemed—and literally was—so far away from where she grew up Down Under. As if everything was imagined, created, or just *happened* somewhere else first. In Australia, it felt like she was experiencing it secondhand.

The glossy images in those dreamy magazine pages became an engine, Laura's desire to be where it happens, the gas in the tank. In high school, and later at university, she hit the phones and wrote the letters (email was years away) to the key publications in Australia's tiny fashion industry. She started interning at any magazine that would have her—the first one was a Sydney style title called *Hero*. She spent most of her time photocopying and getting editors breakfast sandwiches, but, oh baby, she was *in*.

Meanwhile, among the humdrum of public-school life in Woodbridge, Virginia, Kristina's fascination with the fantasy of magazines like *Seventeen*, *Mademoiselle*, and *Vogue* soon found a real-world outlet in the form of her high school newspaper, *The Valkyrie* (her editorial Valhalla). It wasn't long before the newspaper was winning awards, and stories like her investigation into whether the school's Viking mascot was sexist propaganda (it was!) propelled her to the position of coeditor in chief. Every late night she spent tweaking layouts and headlines brought her one step closer to her glossy-page dreams.

Raised with parallel ambitions but geographically worlds apart, Laura and Kristina were bonded by another vital thing: both considered *Sex and the City* to be a seminal documentary.

Cut to 2001. We first met in New York City twenty-four years ago at the Marc Jacobs fashion show at Pier 54, the night before the world changed forever: September 10, 2001. Marc Jacobs was the hottest show in town (still is, actually) and Laura sneaked in with her one New York friend and social fairy godmother, Libby Callaway, who was the fashion editor at *The New York Post*. Laura had just moved to New York from Sydney—packing two suitcases, several pairs of impractical shoes, and, for some reason, two decorative ceramic vases—six days before. She had saved up around $5,000. Allowed to enter the country on a foreign journalist visa, and with approximately 1.5 industry contacts, Laura pinballed around the city, quickly learning how to hustle and who the players were (she almost keeled over when she saw the real Calvin Klein . . . in his own damn store!).

Kristina was more established, one year into her job as a fashion writer at *Harper's Bazaar*. She'd come to *Bazaar* after stints at *New York Magazine*, *Time Out New York* (her first real salaried job, at $26,000 a year), and working as *Sex and the City* writer Candace Bushnell's assistant after cold-calling her in 1996 for an interview from a pay phone near her NYU dorm. Candace, the trailblazing journalist-about-town who documented the glitz, glam, and gritty realities of NYC dating life with her cult-read *New York Observer* column, was in the process of turning those escapades into the TV gold mine that would become HBO's *Sex and the City* (again, our documentary. Stop laughing).

Candace put Kristina to work, tasking her with important jobs like taking her iconic white Tom Ford Gucci dress with the hip cutout to the dry cleaner and transcribing notes she had jotted down the night before on cocktail napkins. All perfect training for fashion magazines, where Kristina, grateful to just be in the room, relished her sixth-row seat at fashion shows (who needs to see full bodies anyway?) and was now living in a whirlwind of creativity, chaos . . . and cosmos.

But back to Marc Jacobs: the pier where the show was held was dark, cavernous, and electric. Laura skittered around on Libby's coattails, wide-eyed, gripping a glass of champagne. There were grapes and wine everywhere (*très* Dionysus), a pool filled with gardenias, a gaggle of supermodels in the wild, and, wait, is-that-Sarah-Jessica-Parker-over-there-holy-shit.

Kristina was sitting at one of the Grape Tables when Laura came by. Both were wearing black, Kristina with narrow, nerdy tortoiseshell glasses. "Ooh," Laura thought, "a Thinker." Kristina's first impression of Laura was that she talked a lot, while Laura thought she was being judged (but, like, in a nice way?). Twenty-four years later, this has not changed.

Over the next two decades, just like those ducks on the pond, we paddled to the top of our industry. Laura's first New York job was a heady six weeks at *Talk* magazine (working for Tina Brown and, *yeesh*, Harvey Weinstein) before it closed while she was on a shoot in LA with shirtless young actors being Photoshopped emerging from ostrich eggs (shout-out to Gabriel Macht from *Suits*; you had it then, and you have it now). She was then hired by *W* magazine—the archly fabulous, mildly bitchy go-to for fashion and society—in 2002, editing writers from the London and Paris bureaus. For some reason, she left for a crappy nine months at *Details*, then finally arrived as articles director at *Harper's Bazaar*—where Kristina was still in residence and had been promoted to fashion features editor.

One of us wrote about dresses, the other about the gals who wore them—or as our indefatigable boss Glenda Bailey would say, "Hemlines and Headlines!"

We both stayed in that high fashion madhouse for years: *Bazaar* was a baptism by fire, whose flame never went out. Kristina rose to executive editor before leaving to become editor in chief of *WSJ. Magazine* in 2012. Over the same period, Laura became executive editor, special projects (concepting shoots, writing stories, booking a zillion covers, and general celebrity whispering) until *InStyle* came calling in 2016.

We did it, damn it! We finally became editors in chief. Yes, that storied, very-weird-when-you-think-about-it title was a big prize. Well, bigger in the *past*. The mythical Town Car era of the '90s was never ours. Budgets got smaller and smaller, and all our going-out looks were either borrowed from designers or liberated from the clothing racks in the office "fashion closet." But because we had hustler DNA, we drove it like we stole it.

Kristina's discerning taste (she was Quiet Luxury before it was a thing), relationships, and business brain (she loves to probe a Euro fashion executive to get all *le thé*) put *WSJ. Magazine* into the fashion industry's frontal lobe. She oversaw all editorial content and "brand extensions" (social media, events, conferences, newsletters, digital desk, and more), which made her News Corp. bosses lots of money.

Kristina loved it all, be it analyzing the texture of paper stock for the print edition or the analytics behind a viral digital piece, and unlike Laura, she did not get an instant headache from looking at an Excel spreadsheet. She also wore and sold a lot of navy three-ply cashmere sweaters.

And just like her sweaters, Kristina was comfy, ensconced in the soft weave of success and routine. She could have stayed in the luxurious folds of *WSJ. Magazine* forever, but in late 2022, just two floors above her, her boss was being replaced. And this would change everything.

Laura started at *InStyle*, a massive but benign Hollywood and fashion instructional mag, in the summer of 2016. She kicked the magazine in the ass—quite literally, launching the Badass Women platform in 2018. When women read *InStyle*, Laura wanted them to feel better about themselves: not worse, not lesser. (Her slogan for the brand: "Everybody's In.") Throughout her time there, Laura ushered *InStyle* vibrantly, and often exhaustedly, through a divisive political landscape, racial unrest, and two enervating years of COVID-19. And while she embraced celebrity and high fashion (her sweaters, FYI, were more sparkly than navy), she also operated from a place of warmth and community.

But by late 2021, magazines were in decline, being gobbled up, Pac-Man-like, by digital and social media. It was also starting to feel a little repetitive; everything revolved around survival, i.e., advertising. And while Laura certainly didn't miss Covid, she missed the times when the work felt more urgent, more important:

providing inspiration and levity to an isolated readership who sorely needed it.

When she was prepping an upcoming cover, she noted that the actress would have to wear Louis Vuitton (both the brand she was on contract with and the biggest money fish in fashion) and the whole machine was returning, once again, to obligation. She loathed what she called "tin cupping," a ritual where you would bow and scrape for a fashion brand's purse holders during the fashion shows in Europe. It was all so démodé.

Her mind had already wandered to other possibilities: starting a beauty company, exploring TV, or just striking out on her own. (She was also an early adopter of Instagram, where she had a strong personal identity and a few hundred thousand followers—extremely helpful if you want to work for yourself.) So, one day she hopped on LegalZoom and registered her own company, LB Media, LLC. LegalZoom mailed her a pleather folder with her business registration stamped on it, and she popped it in a random drawer. She felt, for the first time in her career, that she had insurance.

And Then We Got Canned

LAURA: Cut to February 2022 and . . . womp womp. I got fired first. In late 2021, *InStyle* and its parent company, Meredith, was sold to Dotdash, a digital media company (and the magazine's third owner in five years). The Dotdash dudes settled in for three months, quoted Wu-Tang a lot, and, on one sunny day in early February, closed the print version of *InStyle* and laid off myself and our editorial staff over Zoom.

While I'd read the industry room (for months), it was still a shock. I went full Winston Churchill ("Fear is a reaction, courage is a decision" lite) with the team and spent the rest of the day lying on my bed with my sneakers still on, receiving hundreds of texts and DMs (unlike Churchill). I was so busy being a human auto-reply to concerned friends and colleagues that I didn't even start drinking. (Don't worry, I got to it.)

The official terminology in the Dotdash Meredith press release and following news pickup was "Laura Brown was terminated." (Sadly, I missed the new word du jour that refers to media firings: "defenestrated." It means being thrown out of a window. I originally thought it meant "disemboweled." Never too old to learn!)

For my termination, there were no killer robots, just a robotic HR representative telling me she was sending over some paperwork to sign—and when my health insurance would end (*fuuuck*). I remember making some dumb, self-preserving jokes and wondering if I needed a lawyer. But who? I'd never needed a lawyer for anything!

Publicly, I said nothing apart from posting an Instagram Story of my hand holding a Sausage McMuffin (this was not my salmon and spinach era) and saying I'd get back to people when I could.

I went to that drawer and pulled out my LB Media folder. I knew I had a valuable currency in the industry as myself—not as *InStyle*. Most importantly, I knew I had enough LB juice to not just *be* myself, but work *for* myself, too. I'd been captive to the fickleness and self-made drama of publishing for almost three damn decades, and I never wanted a boss to be able to control my mood, my day, or my life ever again.

KRISTINA: Over a year later, in April 2023, I had a spidey sense that something was not right at the *WSJ* mother ship when I couldn't get an introductory meeting on the books with my new boss... for three months. The meeting was finally confirmed, set to take place in her office, but five minutes before, it was moved to the HR department. My fate was sealed: "I'm sorry we have to meet under these circumstances," she said. My ten-year run as editor in chief of *WSJ. Magazine* was over in ten minutes.

The boss said she'd follow my lead on the narrative around my leaving. "The narrative?" I replied, my voice sharp with disbelief. I wasn't embezzling money, for Christ's sake. I had zero desire to spin some half-baked, PR-friendly version of events to save face. I'd given a decade of my life to this place, and I wasn't about to obscure the fact that this was their decision, not mine. (Why would I leave my dream job?) "You can tell everyone you fired me," I said with as much composure as I could muster. And so, the next day, she did.

Despite not having regained my wits, I still had the foresight to demand the company pay for a tequila-soaked bye-bye bash. Laura had jokes, but I had... vision.

LAURA: Kristina texted me, "Getting the boot. Call me when you're up." Now, Kristina is pragmatic to a fault, but she was in shock. I just tried to be helpful: I was further along on Fired Road, still alive, not broke, flashlight at the ready.

I called Kristina, and after we talked a lot about employment lawyers—we were in senior roles, had never been fired before, and were being pushed a ton of brain-melting paperwork—I launched into my trusty public service announcement, which

I'd been rattling away for months to friends, colleagues, and reporters: "Your equity isn't attached to your job. It's *yours*. It doesn't go *poof* when your circumstances change." We both knew this implicitly, despite being rightly pissed that we'd lost our jobs.

KRISTINA: I've always been more of a "company girl." I enjoy structure, strategy, and all the grown-up things. (My favorite number is 401(k).) I thrive in that environment, finding energy and security in well-defined roles and goals. So, frankly, thank God Laura got fired first (our friends, laughing quite hard, concurred). She emerged from the experience resilient, unfazed, and just . . . happier. Her journey post-*InStyle* and the way she metabolized it showed me that there was life beyond setbacks.

When I wasn't alternately texting Laura and my lawyer about my severance package, I was carpet-bombing every corner of my professional network, setting up meeting after meeting. Determination + slight panic = motivation! Reading the room became my new superpower. I gauged the shifting dynamics and potential opportunities and asserted occasionally wobbly control amid the chaos. Every conversation, every connection, every idea exchanged provided me with a pathway forward. I also napped in my navy sweaters—a lot.

I wasn't entirely sure what I was looking for—it wasn't as though the handful of other magazines I might have wanted to edit were suddenly going to fall into my lap (Happy forty-second anniversary at Condé Nast, Anna Wintour!). I was open to something different, but I also felt like I needed someone to tap me on the shoulder and point me in the right direction.

I loved reading, I loved culture, I loved fashion, I loved telling stories—and, yes, I loved telling people what to do. But I loved the sheer craft of making magazines: it was like handpainting frescoes in an age of Photoshop.

I've always thought of myself as an entrepreneurial person (despite only working for mega organizations). But I was always hustling and pushing to build something new. I didn't want to spend my days managing decline (i.e., traditional magazines that relied on ad revenue). I wanted to create, not maintain. So, whatever came next had to feel dynamic and full of possibility.

Later that month, Laura and Kristina met for a drink with a friend at the wildly upscale Centurion New York club (where people put down black American Express cards, not the green ones we both had to return along with our company badges). On the

Uber ride there, Laura texted Kristina: "OK, here's what we're gonna do. We're going to take an Insta picture together, look really cute, and caption it, 'All the cool girls get fired.'"

We'd been up front with friends, colleagues, and the whole fashion industry that we'd been canned, so why not tell the world? We were great at what we did, and we got fired. So what? We didn't realize, at the time, just how subversive that post would be.

(Here's the pic below. Plus, look at all that wine above our credit limit!)

Getting Our Shit Together

People often say that getting fired is the best thing to happen to you, and while you might want to punch them in the face, they're kind of right. Guess what: when you look out from your career sandpit, wouldn't you know it, there's a whole beach! (You've likely been in that sandpit too long anyway, and a dog probably pooped in it.)

LAURA: As my husband, Brandon, is fond of telling me, I've been Johnny Appleseed throughout my career, guilelessly flinging seeds around in vaster and vaster fields. And I have to say, after doing a bit of a Fired Tour of Manhattan to give industry folks all the gossip right after being canned, I didn't really call anybody or pitch anybody—and thankfully, I had enough personal security (both mentally and, for a little while, financially) to not go full panic-pants. I was just about to get married, and my mom was unwell (thankfully better now), so I was like a dog with its head stuck out the car window, looking at the world racing by, wondering what would come my way. Rightly or wrongly, I've never been a read-the-instructions kinda girl.

While working for myself started out as rickety as an old roller coaster (see the following chapters on health care, money, and all the other post-firing terrors), and sometimes was slow going, it's been both freeing and thrilling. I own my own business now: fashion, film, nonprofit, TV, design, and advising startups where I might make Actual Real Money—not to mention this book, which is somehow becoming a business.

An important thing to note: media is no longer linear, and its future is personality based. Just look at all the journalists leaving legacy media behind and starting Substacks, podcasts, and YouTube channels. Each of us is a magazine now, broadcasting our opinions, likes, dislikes, and trends on various platforms. *You are the brand.* I do some projects where I am "the talent" (with fashion brands or in TV development) and some as a consultant, like my work with the global HIV nonprofit (RED) and lifestyle startups. I've taken to calling myself the Lightbulb Lady, because all sorts of companies and brands come to me for ideas that, hopefully, will impact the culture. For better, not worse.

What is also *infinitely* better is being in control of where I am and when I'm available. (A walk in Central Park at 3 p.m. on a Tuesday? Why not? Just do a command performance on Zooms at either end.)

My husband and I don't have kids, so I'm the first to acknowledge we have a lighter financial lift than so many others in that regard, but I am still the breadwinner of my household and I help my mom out in Australia, too. And while money still needs to come in (we live in New York City!), I realized my skill set can work in much broader industries than just fashion. And what do you know: it's a helluva lot more interesting, opening the door to the big wide world.

Oh, and after over thirty years in the media, I know what I'm worth.

KRISTINA: They say that a girl's gotta have options, and boy, did I take that saying to heart. I refused to constrict myself to the narrow confines of defeat or self-pity. Instead, I embraced the uncertainty and channeled my nervous energy into exploring a multitude of possibilities, from consulting to in-house options at companies I'd covered as a journalist but hadn't spent two decades inside. The world was suddenly a vast playground of potential, and I was ready to embrace it.

And it's the same for *all* professional women; we just have to get out of our old habits, broaden our minds, and even take meetings with people whom, a month ago, we might have either brushed off or been too scared to ask. For me and my partner, Magnus, living in the Greatest City in the World means managing a never-ending list of expenses: rent, food, school tuitions for my kids, and those little luxuries, like Pilates, that, post-firing, suddenly seemed like massive indulgences. But even with blunt financial reality staring me in the face, I remained stubbornly optimistic. This was a chance to redefine what success looks like, broaden my professional landscape, and embrace the many opportunities that change inevitably brings. Of course, I wobbled occasionally—who doesn't?—but I kept my eyes on the horizon rather than my navel.

And then, almost six months to the day I left *WSJ*... I got hired. One of the first people who called me after I got the boot was Charles F. Stewart, the CEO of Sotheby's. I respected his vision (we had covered him and Sotheby's at *WSJ*) and knew him a little bit socially. Charlie was a fan of what I had built at *WSJ* and asked me to consider coming to Sotheby's.

Like I said earlier, I'm a company girl. I'm not remotely built for freelance life, though I did flirt with the idea of setting up a consulting firm called Unsolicited Advice. My partner is a freelance creative director, and I couldn't picture the both of us navigating the gig grind—I just don't have the pitching-and-chasing (and invoicing!) chip in me.

The more I thought about it, though, the more intriguing Sotheby's became. The opportunity to set up a media division and relaunch *Sotheby's Magazine* was too good to pass up. Despite the challenges of the publishing industry, I'm not done making magazines. I also love working for a long-established institution (my most recent employers are 281, 135, and 158 years old). There's a certain magic in working within hallowed halls. And it makes me feel young. Our courtship continued, and I started at Sotheby's in January 2024.

Then We Wrote This Book

All the Cool Girls Get Fired (yes, named after that pivotal Instagram post) is less a how-to book and more of a guide to help you recognize and embrace your skills, your equity, and your worth. We will help you determine which next move is worthy of you and what you have to offer. Most importantly, this book is a mindset shift—a pragmatic, empowering, and humorous (hey, you gotta laugh) way to make lemonade from lemons.

We wrote this book for women at all stages of their careers because, let's face it, the corporate ladder was not originally designed with us in mind. It's inherently harder for women to get to the top, so when you fall—or are pushed—from your slippery rung, the landing is, you guessed it, *harder*. This challenge isn't just for those in high-powered positions; it's a reality faced by many women as they navigate industries that, given they were constructed by men, weren't made for us in the first place.

And you know how everyone refers to the fabled "C-Suite"? Well, a key reminder that the *C* comes from the word "chief." And guess what: the first chiefs of industry were not women. These days, *C* is in CEO, CFO, COO, CTO, CMO, CIO . . . the business version of military rank. And all of those C's? They are still mostly men.

As of 2025, things have improved somewhat, but women are still in the vast minority. In their tenth annual "Women in the Workplace" study, Sheryl Sandberg's Lean In organization and McKinsey & Company reported that the number of women in the C-Suite in the United States had increased from 17 percent in 2015 to 29 percent in 2024. White women hold 22 percent of C-Suite roles, while women of color hold just 7 percent. (The report explains, "Women of color have experienced larger relative gains over the past several years. But given their significant under-representation to start, they still have a long way to go to reach parity with white women.")

So, while there have been gains, here's the rub: the study revealed that the majority of those roles aren't that of CEO—aren't the boss—but more often in support positions/career cul-de-sacs like chief human resources officer. Is that because us girls just *love* to chat? (Frown emoji.)

And while we're here in the pit, when it comes to workplace gender parity, the report estimated that white women will only achieve parity with men by 2046, while women of color won't get there until 2074. It might be easier to colonize the moon.

BUT. And this is a big, *big* but... just like in our business—media—the definition of work *itself* is no longer linear. Why does this "Chief Suite" need to be the goal, anyway? The whole thing has the faint but growing ring of datedness to it—a definition of success that hasn't shifted since the postwar era. (You know, since Mad Men were drinking three martinis at lunch and having heart attacks at the table.)

Over here, you see, we're a little more *lean out*. The argument of this entire book is that the corner office is not all there is. Real power comes from individualism. And guess what helps you come to this realization? Being fired.

Being fired is a universal experience and one of the greatest equalizers because *everyone* feels the same: like shit (regardless of how much money they might have). And while it may feel like getting fired is just happening to you, that you're all alone, that people are whispering about you, that you will forever be branded with a Scarlet *F*... guess what? It isn't, you aren't, they aren't, you won't.

For all women, the feeling of shame—the *great unmooring*—is the same. And for some reason, unlike men, women tend to take that great big ball of shame and carry it around with them. We're constantly mystified as to why, because, man, that shame is heavy. (And no one asked you to pick up the damn thing anyway.)

But remember! You are a vital part of a rich tapestry of awesome, accomplished ladies—in all fields, of all incomes—who have also hit that bump in the road and, after a brief slowdown, changed gears and accelerated into a brilliant future.

We hope the Cool Girl stories in this book inspire you and remind you of all you have earned—and learned. Every woman we interviewed—many of whom you know from the media, Hollywood, fashion, finance, or activism—has a different, and vital, learning to share. After they were fired, some trusted their instincts. Others briefly took a lesser role and earned their way back. Some took the time gained from losing their job to focus on a long-dormant passion. Some lost companies they helped build, and, for a time, their identity, too. Others were publicly humiliated. One of them gets fired *all the time*. And *every one* of them had all the same feelings that you are going through right now.

So, we hope reading these stories makes you stand a little taller and pound your chest, because there is a world of options for you if you just take a breath and look.

Our biggest hope is that this book will unify and reassure the younger and older, the richer, the poorer, the connected, and the isolated (no more of that, by the way—didn't we just tell you how you're not alone?). The most important thing to remember is that you have a real community, both in these pages and out there, with other women in the working world. Our growing Cool Girl universe leads with honesty, frankness, and the word we *all* work so hard toward: *ownership*.

Also, in case we haven't been clear, this is fine to read while drinking. In fact, we recommend it. If you're into that.

1

Your Money

How to Stretch Your Severance and Minimize Expenses

Being in an industry known for having great perks (yay, free lipstick!) and lousy pay (but you get free lipstick?), we had the good fortune of being in well-compensated positions. Well, not compared to Goldman Sachs, but better than a poke in the eye. As part of our "termination agreements," we received severance packages that provided a few months of a financial cushion while we tried to figure out how to continue to cover the bills.

Laura was shelling out for her upcoming wedding in Hawaii, now perfectly timed because she didn't have any work to do — but also had zero income coming in afterward. This confluence of a joyful thing (love!) and a hugely stressful thing (money!) was something else. After years of a reassuring biweekly salary deposit, watching her bank balance steadily decrease was like the Sunday Scaries, but seven days a week. She just willed herself that she was going to be OK, reminding herself of all the professional equity she'd earned. Surely equity would equal . . . equity?!

For Kristina, who has two children, this meant recalibrating financial plans and priorities. Suddenly, every expense required microscopic scrutiny (fewer Ubers/more subways; pressing pause on Pilates and lunging around the living room), while the need to stretch her severance as far as possible became paramount. It was a total recalibration, rethinking the value of money and the importance of planning ahead, underscored by the urgency to find new income before the safety net unraveled and she fell out. Plop.

If you're laid off, be it suddenly or something you saw coming, money is likely your first concern, and rightfully so. First off, take a breath and look at your bank account, your savings, and your 401(k) (or pension equivalent if you are based outside of the United States), if you have one. What are you still due from your former employer, if anything, and how long will that last you? What are your expenses? How long can you live on the money you have? (This does not include putting stuff on credit cards "to pay later": don't even look at that toxic plastic.) Are unemployment benefits available to you? Do you have rich parents? Kidding. We don't.

But let's start on D Day—or F(ired) Day.

Review Your Severance

A severance package is typically one to two weeks of pay for every year you were employed (so, if you are fired after five years, you should receive five to ten weeks of salary). For executive positions, this might be higher (six to twelve months), while in lower-paid industries, you might just be offered a flat amount. In the US, there is no federal law that requires severance to be paid. But if you have a contract, a good relationship with your former employer, or a potential unlawful termination case, they will likely cough up.*

Cut to: you sitting down with your severance offer (and likely in a full-blown financial panic). The most important thing to remember is that you don't have to sign any sort of agreement either in person or as soon as HR sends it to you. It may not feel like it, but the ball is in your court. Ron Lieber, Your Money columnist for *The New York Times*, says, "There's no downside to saying absolutely nothing. It's not always easy or possible; some people are more prone to emotions than others, and unexpected feelings may pop up if this has never happened to you before."

That said, if you can keep it together, "Take it in. See what paperwork is being put in front of you in terms of a separation package." And put on your big-girl pants: "They may want

---

* This will vary according to where you live, so check the legislation where you are based. In the United Kingdom, for example, if your role has been made redundant, you will be entitled to statutory redundancy pay which will be based on length of service and your age. In other countries like the Netherlands, you will be offered a transition payment that is calculated on years of service and salary. Now is the time to geek out about these things and do your research!

you to sign some kind of nondisclosure or non-disparagement agreement—or agree to a separation package. *You don't have to do that.* These are not evaporating offers. You are not required to sign anything right away."

Repeat: *the offer will not evaporate.* Lieber adds, "It's very rare that if you say to someone laying you off, 'I'm not prepared to sign paperwork right here. I'm going to take this away and think about it,' that they'll say, 'Well, that severance will be gone tomorrow, so you have to sign it.'" You have some time.

Negotiate, Negotiate, Negotiate

Whatever amount is offered, you should consider it your worst-case scenario—you have absolutely zero to lose by asking for more. (What are they going to do—fire you?)

"Ask for a better deal," says Lieber. "Maybe it's money, maybe it's 'Keep me on the books long enough to get tuition reimbursement for this course that I wanted to take anyway that may help me with my pivot.' Maybe it's reimbursement for career counseling.

"Or maybe it's time that you need: 'Please keep me on the payroll even if it means taking my salary down to a dollar so that I can have this surgery in three weeks while I still have health insurance.'" (Depressing, but pragmatic for you U.S.-based readers out there.) "You can just ask for longer health insurance even if you were not on the payroll for very long. The advantage of walking away from the severance being offered and thinking about it for twenty-four hours is that you can make a list of the things to ask for."

Some ideas for your list:

- Vacation time payout. Ensure that all accrued vacation time is fully paid out.

- Outplacement services. Request that the company covers employment-related services such as career coaching, résumé/bio writing, interview practice, and job placement assistance.

- Noncompete clause. If your work agreement includes a noncompete clause, ask your former employer to reduce its duration. It's an easy lift for them and gets you back in the job market sooner.

- Keep company-issued property. Request to keep company-issued items like your computer or cell phone, as they often have minimal value to the company but can still be useful to you. (Those iPhone 8s still work—just ask Laura's mom.)

- Health insurance coverage. If you need continued health insurance for a specific reason (e.g., an upcoming surgery), negotiate for extended coverage in lieu of part or all of your severance package. You could say, "I'm happy to sign this non-disparagement agreement as long as my health insurance lasts long enough for me to get this surgery." The company may prioritize this request over severance, giving you leverage.

Lieber adds, "The employer is not going to want to create more bad blood than is necessary. They understand that if they treat you humanely, you're not going to go out and say terrible things about them. If you're in a situation that could inspire some sympathy, go back and explain what it is. 'My child has really complicated health problems. I'm taking care of a parent with dementia. I am struggling with this or that health challenge. Can you please just do X or Y; it would mean a lot to me and create a lot of goodwill.'"

That means not just goodwill with you, but for all the myriad people you are going to talk to about it. It's just a better look for everyone, all around. "They're not going to take the deal off the table if you politely ask for something better," Lieber argues, "so why wouldn't you try?"

How Long Will Your Severance Last?

Sit down and figure out your bottom-line monthly costs. (Your friends can take you out for drinks, so no need to count that. Do your best doped-up Kristen Wiig in *Bridesmaids*: "Help me, I'm poor.")

"Do the calculations to see how long it will last just covering basic expenses," says financial expert Jennifer Barrett, author of *Think Like a Breadwinner: A Wealth-Building Manifesto for Women Who Want to Earn More (and Worry Less)*. "Pull your debit and credit card statements to get an understanding of what you've spent in different categories—rent or mortgage, recurring bills, groceries, toiletries." Then average out your variable expenses: dinners out, the new shoes you bought, "to get an understanding of what that average is over the past three to six months. Then you know how long your severance can cover at least your basic needs without having to touch your savings."

Once you've worked out how far your severance will go—even if it's just a couple of weeks—you'll feel better, because you've been responsible and done the math. You are owning your circumstances and getting your power back. Barrett adds, "Now you can take a breath and start putting together a strategy to find a new job and bring in new sources of income."

Do You Have an Emergency Fund?

OK, first, *do not let this headline freak you out*. We've all had jobs that barely paid—borrowing from a roommate to get through the end of the month. It's tough out there, ladies!

Most financial advisers recommend having three to six months' worth of an emergency fund. So, if you have one, good for you. "The benefit to having a financial runway or savings in these moments is that you don't have to make knee-jerk decisions," says finance expert and host of the *So Money* podcast Farnoosh Torabi. "You don't feel like you have to immediately start frantically applying for work. You can take a minute and think, 'OK, what did I like about my job? What did I not like?'"

But if you don't, there's no need to panic. Instead, identify your "last resort" money. Lieber says, "If you don't have an emergency fund, you should not be ashamed. Ask yourself, 'What's my emergency fund *now*?' What are your sources of income? If severance and unemployment run out and you can't get any side gigs or project work, what is your last resort?"

Back to our rich parents joke: perhaps there is a relative or a friend who is more solvent than you and can offer you a loan.

"You probably don't want to take them up on that right after a job loss, but [if time passed] would you take a low-interest loan or a no-interest loan?" Lieber says. "Maybe you would."

It also pays to look around: there could be money to be made by selling or refinancing something you own—from a handbag to your home. If you own your home, "Open a home equity line of credit when you do have income, so you don't have to ask for it after you've lost your job," Lieber says. "Then it's just sitting there. You could use that potentially as an emergency fund."

Do you have a 401(k) (or a pension equivalent depending on where you are based)? Does your partner? If straits are dire, you could borrow from your retirement savings, which you'll pay back with interest into your account. Alternatively, you can make a withdrawal, but this permanently reduces your retirement funds and comes with taxes and penalties, especially if you're under fifty-nine and a half. Hardship withdrawals are available for specific urgent needs like medical bills or preventing eviction, but they also come with potential tax implications.

According to the IRS, most IRAs (individual retirement arrangements) allow the following: "The maximum amount a participant may borrow from [their] plan is 50% of [their] vested account balance or $50,000, whichever is less. An exception to this limit is if 50% of the vested account balance is less than $10,000: in such a case, the participant may borrow up to $10,000."*

---

* Your circumstances will vary according to where you are based of course. We would always recommend you seek out professional financial advice from an accredited expert who can advise you on the best plan of action.

Of course, there are strings: "Plan sponsors may require an employee to repay the full outstanding balance of a loan if [they terminate] employment or if the plan is terminated. If the employee is unable to repay the loan, the employer will treat it as a distribution and report it to the IRS on Form 1099-R. The employee can avoid the immediate income tax consequences by rolling over all or part of the loan's outstanding balance to an IRA or eligible retirement plan by the due date (including extensions) for filing the Federal income tax return for the year in which the loan is treated as a distribution."

Translation: If you've previously taken a 401(k) loan and are laid off, you'll have to pay it back immediately. If you can't, that distribution is taxable and you'll pay a 10 percent penalty.

A real last resort: you can cash in your 401(k) after a layoff, but one, you'll be taxed up the wazoo (income tax, state tax, a 10 percent early withdrawal penalty), and two, you cannot borrow against it.

So, unless your world is turning to ash, do not do this.

Got a headache, yet? Us, too. But having all this stuff written down will save you many more headaches in the future. "It's less thinking about the emergency fund for day one, but the sources of an emergency fund for day 257," says Lieber. "That's reassuring, knowing you won't be out on the street. It's a psychological backstop."

So, take an Advil and be proud of yourself.

Apply for Unemployment ASAP

It's easy to forget, while freaking out about all the things you have to *pay for*, that, for some time at least, the government will *pay you*. All the taxes that have come out of your salary for however long you've been working? They go toward this, so don't be shy or ashamed about filing for unemployment. Be mercenary—this is America! (This attitude also works globally, trust us. Look into what jobseeker support your government provides, and take advantage of it.)

"I'm always surprised by the number of people who just forget about unemployment insurance or feel guilty about it," says Lieber. "You're paying taxes, and those taxes are for everyone, including you, who ends up in this situation. So, file for the damn check."

Filing for unemployment is a complex process, so get going ASAP so money starts coming in. "It'll almost certainly be more than a thousand dollars a month," Lieber says. "It might even be over two thousand dollars a month. So take it."

Torabi says, "Applying for unemployment insurance right away is very important because sometimes there's a backlog before they start paying you. But even if your payment doesn't start for three weeks, they will backdate it."

In the United States, unemployment benefits differ from state to state (that was news to us, as was most of this chapter). There is *not* a federal unemployment program. Visit usa.gov/unemployment-benefits to learn more about what you're eligible for in your state.

Important: if you are fired for cause, this may reduce your chance of receiving benefits. It depends on the circumstances of your firing and the unemployment laws in your state.

Most states' unemployment benefits offer "temporary, partial income replacement" to employees who:

- Lost their jobs through no fault of their own or are working reduced hours.

- Are looking for work and are able/available to work.

- Have worked long enough to establish a claim.

What differs from state to state:

- Duration of benefits. Most are twenty-six weeks, but some states like Massachusetts give you thirty weeks, and others, like South Carolina, give you twenty.

- Qualifications. This could be the length of time you were employed, the amount you earned during your tenure, the reason you became unemployed, and your availability and ability to work again. Each state has its own specific rules to determine who qualifies.

- Average weekly benefit amount. Some states have a weekly average of $447 (Washington) whereas others have a weekly average of $192 (Louisiana).

You can file for unemployment online or on the phone. To find your state's unemployment website, visit the usa.gov link or google "(YOUR STATE) + unemployment." (Make sure you are giving your info to a website with a .gov address, because there are scams out there.)

Here's a New York State example (we were fired here so it's as good as any):

- If you were laid off/fired in New York, you can file for unemployment if you worked in New York within the last eighteen months, and you can receive up to twenty-six weeks of benefits. Your benefits exist in the form of a weekly payment and are based on your past wages. Per nyc.gov, a typical range of weekly benefits is $100 to $500 per week. This income is taxable.

- Some states will have a benefits calculator that you can use to try to estimate your payments. New York State's is https://ux.labor.ny.gov/benefit-rate-calculator/.

For example: Say you were laid off in March 2025 in New York State with a salary of $100,000. New York calculates weekly unemployment benefits as 1/26th of your highest quarter earnings, the maximum cap $504 per week.

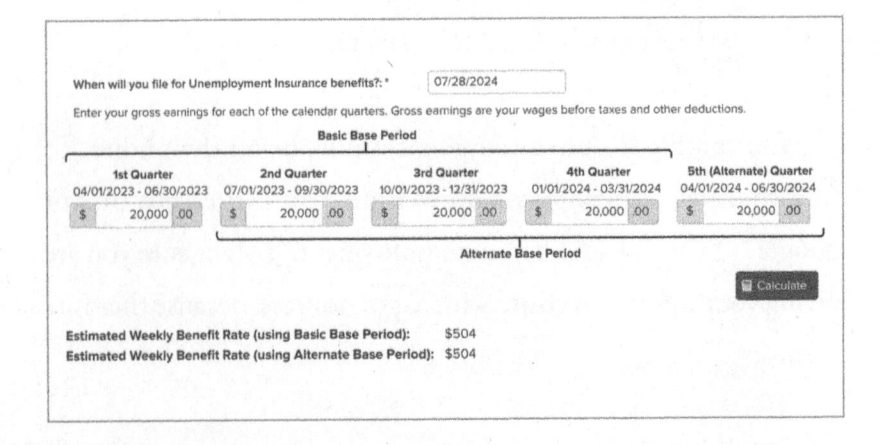

When will you file for Unemployment Insurance benefits?: * 07/28/2024

Enter your gross earnings for each of the calendar quarters. Gross earnings are your wages before taxes and other deductions.

Basic Base Period

1st Quarter	2nd Quarter	3rd Quarter	4th Quarter	5th (Alternate) Quarter
04/01/2023 - 06/30/2023	07/01/2023 - 09/30/2023	10/01/2023 - 12/31/2023	01/01/2024 - 03/31/2024	04/01/2024 - 06/30/2024
$ 20,000 .00	$ 20,000 .00	$ 20,000 .00	$ 20,000 .00	$ 20,000 .00

Alternate Base Period

🗑 Calculate

Estimated Weekly Benefit Rate (using Basic Base Period): $504
Estimated Weekly Benefit Rate (using Alternate Base Period): $504

Nationally, New York is somewhat in the middle, with Mississippi offering the lowest cap of $235 per week and Massachusetts the highest cap at $1,033 per week. Most states will notify you of your outcome and benefit determination three to four weeks after you apply.

So, get thee to thy specific state's website, or whatever national government website applies to you international folks, read the instructions, and get your money! One key thing to remember: unemployment benefits are not free cash; they are income, and will be taxed. According to Sofia Figueroa, senior financial planner at Ellevest, "Consider setting part of the unemployment checks aside for your eventual tax bill. If you can't do that because you need to make ends meet, just keep it in the back of your mind that at some point that's going to come back. When you file your taxes the following year, that's considered income."

Pause Investments

During this time in between jobs, it might be wise to stop contributing to things like your IRA or your children's 529 college savings program, or any other personal investments. If you're signed up for automatic deductions, you can contact the financial institutions managing your investment funds to pause or adjust contributions. There is usually no penalty for pausing contributions, but you'll want to keep the annual contribution limit in mind if you intend to catch up later. This will delay your savings goal but will take the edge off while you sort out your finances. You can always resume contributions when you're more financially stable.

Make Some Quick Money (Legally)

If you don't have that three-to-six-month cash runway, what work can you pick up? And don't get all caught up on whether something is "beneath you." You know what's beneath you? Not being able to pay your rent. And, hell, any grunt job makes for great stories when it comes time to write your memoir!

"Realistically, it's not about *'How can I save more?'* but *'How can I earn?'* You've got to pull that lever instead," says Torabi. "This isn't about applying to replace your full-time job. Of course you are thinking about that, but also you could find a ten-hour job here, a fifteen-hour job there."

Think of it as a side hustle (even if there's nothing it's on the side of at this very moment). "Leverage your existing skill set. Look online," Torabi advises. Maybe you were an accountant but make a killer cappuccino, so, go be a barista for a minute (think of all the friends you'll make!). "Maybe you speak another language or you are really great at teaching—you could tutor a subject that you were really great at in school. Some of us think that's so beneath us, and we're like, *I'm a professional*. But check out sites that have these part-time freelance roles; I would immediately plug into that."

Marianne Ruggiero, founder of Optima Careers, says, "If you have to take a job right away, sign up with a temp agency, get some cash coming in, post yourself up on Upwork [a job network that connects employers to freelancers], and try to get some project work that you could bang out while you're looking for a job." Sites like Fiverr also let you tap into project-based work, offering gigs for everything from design to writing to voice-overs. It's quick cash and lets you monetize skills you already have.

Back at the bank, move some of your severance into a high-yield account to earn faster. "Put money into a high-yield savings account, especially early on, even if it's small amounts, because that interest will compound," says Jennifer Barrett. Figueroa agrees: "While interest rates are higher, you're going to get a nice little return every month on the money that's sitting there. Even if that's an extra fifty dollars a month, that's fifty dollars a month, right?"

Don't Just Negotiate Severance, Negotiate Everything

Laura was once pondering—well, whining about—why she and her husband, Brandon, were paying so much for cable. So, Brandon called up Spectrum's customer retention department and asked for a new bundle at a better deal. Wouldn't you know it; they gave him one. In an era of so much competition, companies want to keep your business. And there's never any harm in asking.

Credit Card Debt

Lieber says, "If you're in credit card debt, call the company and say, 'Hey, I just got laid off. I'm going to continue to make this minimum payment. And as you know'—if this is true—'I have a really good credit score. I want to stay with your company for decades. Is there anything you can do to give me a temporary or permanent break on the interest so I don't have to take my business elsewhere to a card with a lower interest rate?' That takes fifteen minutes of your time."

Rent

Ask for a break on your rent, too. Remember the Covid rent relief? "All sorts of people got all sorts of breaks during the pandemic," Lieber says. "Plenty of landlords are sympathetic. If you're the only one asking for a break right now, maybe they're likely to be even more sympathetic than they were in 2020."

"Your landlord likes to have reliable renters," says Torabi. "So, for them to have to see you go, hire an agent, find a new resident... that costs them money. Go to them and say, 'Hey, I would love to renegotiate my lease. I got laid off and I have money, but I want to be conservative and careful. If you're up for renewal, could I get a discount or waive some of the fees? Or if I'm willing to pay a few months up front, can we get a discount?' It's always helpful to come up with your own suggestions first to get their wheels turning; then maybe they'll offer you something."

Tuition

"You might be surprised," Torabi says. "Whether it's your child's college or day care, call and say, 'I'm letting you know that we are experiencing financial hardship.' See how they might be able to give you a discount or freeze your account. The school might say, 'Oh, we actually have this scholarship that you can qualify for, or you should reapply for the FAFSA (Free Application for Federal Student Aid) and update your financial information.' It might qualify you for more aid.

"If you're experiencing financial hardship as a result of a layoff, then it's important to let people know before things get out of hand and you miss a bill or it's too late and there's really no more money. There's all sorts of creative ways to address people's financial hardships, but you won't know that until you let them know."

Health and Fitness

Lieber says to ask for a break there, too. "Mental health is often more readily under siege the first couple of weeks after a layoff. So, if exercise is the thing that keeps you sane more than anything else, ask your trainer—if that's how you get your exercise—for a break." You can also sign up for online classes, see what's free on YouTube—hell, go check out some fitness influencer on Instagram and do some free squats.

Student Loans

"If you have student loans and you're experiencing financial hardship, you want to call your lender and see if there's a way that you can get on a deferment, or you can maybe suspend those payments for a while," says Torabi. "It'll probably accrue interest, but at least you'll be able to keep your head above water."

Cut Down on Your Household Expenses

Hey, here's a silver lining to being jobless and a little crestfallen—you're staying in more! While you're home, take stock of your expenses. What are you paying for, subscribing to, or indulging in that you *really, really* need right now? You want to stay home and binge the telly? Keep your streaming (but downgrade to an ad-supported tier). You want to get out of town? Then cancel it.

Find the right equation that makes sure you still live sufficiently, but responsibly.

Now is the time to cancel unnecessary expenses. "Go through your credit or debit card statements and cancel what you won't really miss," says Lieber. Audit subscriptions and memberships you don't need. Are you still paying for a fitness app you downloaded in lockdown? Let go of that meal-kit subscription. What about your magazines, music, extra streaming services, and things on auto subscribe? Do you *really* need more vitamins right now?

Kristina's Apple News subscription offers all the magazines she was receiving in print for one bundled price. Anything she had to read in print she borrowed from the library. Those ten-thousand-word *The New Yorker* stories are an eye killer on a screen. If you can share with a partner, family member, or roommate, consolidate where possible. Start with your Amazon Prime and Spotify accounts and your cell phone plan.

Lieber adds, "That feels empowering because it's something you can do right away and see immediate results. And the more you can cut your burn rate, the more breathing room you have to really think about what you want."

Right Now, Your Credit Card Is Evil

These days, it seems like all you have to do is walk out your front door and with a ping here, a tap there . . . fifty bucks just gone. While these are all speedy and convenient ways to pay for things, they can result in a swift—and inconvenient—accruing of credit card debt, without you even noticing.

"You should never put something on your credit card that you couldn't just pay for in cash that week," says Barrett. "You should never be using it as an alternative because you don't have enough cash on hand to pay for something. That's where you start to really get into trouble."

If you don't pay your credit card bill in full every month, the balance accrues interest, which compounds over time. "In some cases, you can end up paying more in interest than you do for the amount that you borrowed on your credit card."

If you do have a credit card with a high interest rate or are racking up credit card balances, "You could consider trying to do a balance transfer offer or a new credit card that has a promotional period for 0 percent," says Figueroa. "Just remember when that promotional period ends to pay it off or transfer the balance to another 0 percent card; otherwise, the interest rate goes up 20 to 30 percent."

So, take your tap-to-pay cards off your phone and keep your credit card in a drawer, not in your wallet.

Using Cash Saves You Money

When Barrett was writing *Think Like a Breadwinner*, she prioritized using cash. "Once a week I went to the ATM, took out cash, put it in an envelope, and started going food shopping with cash instead of a credit card or Apple Pay. It's really fascinating what happens mentally because you are *über* aware of how much everything costs when you've brought, let's say, forty or sixty dollars to pick up a few groceries. You don't want to get to the cash register and not have enough money to cover it. Just the thought of all these people stuck behind you is enough of an incentive to do the math! Look at every item you're picking up and question whether you need it or not. I found that I spent probably 25 percent less when I used cash because I was so conscientious about what I was buying."

Thrifty *and* nifty! So maybe you skipped the overpriced chocolate-covered cashews, but you'll feel kind of... noble?

Be Honest About Finances with Friends

Now is not the time to try to keep up with the Joneses. Trust us, the whole world is not talking about how they didn't see you at that cool restaurant last week. And your real friends will be there for you—fiscally or otherwise—no matter what.

Don't let your pride get in the way of these conversations. "What's scarier: your ego getting bruised or being broke?" says Torabi.

Barrett remembers, "Ten years ago, one of my closest friends lost her job, and it took her a little while to find another one. She was pretty open about it. She told me and our other close friends, 'Listen, I'm in between jobs; I really can't spend a lot of money, but it's important to me that we still spend time together. So wherever we can save money going out, please, let's do that.'

"We would look for happy hour specials and do whatever we could do to try to cut the bill. About a month into it, another friend and I were talking about it, and we said, 'We're saving money and we're still seeing her, and so we're benefiting, too.' A lot of people will experience periods where they are not bringing in an income. It could be you this time, it could be another friend of yours another time."

Also, your friends have resources that aren't just financial. Torabi mentions the "loud budgeting" movement on TikTok. "It's about goals and being vocal. If you're experiencing financial hardship and you want to find ways to save, talk to your friends about it because they might have resources for you. They might be like, 'Oh hey, my mom's a professional coach or a scout. She can help you find a job for free,' or, 'Let's not eat out for the next month but we can have dinners at each other's houses.' It's important to stay social when you can often feel really lonely."

Too much time on your own isn't great even *when* you're employed, so make sure to manage that inevitable sinking feeling by keeping at least one social event a week on the calendar. It will get you out of your sweatpants, and, even better, out of your head.

Finally, and most importantly: remember, our financially challenged friend, it won't be like this forever. We promise.

2

Lisa Kudrow

Lisa Kudrow is a multi-award-winning comedic actress, best known for playing Phoebe Buffay on *Friends* (1994–2004). She was fired from the role of Roz in the pilot episode of *Frasier* in 1993.

> "I think we're allowed to choose how we see the world. We frame what the experience is."

What Happened

Getting cast on *Frasier* was the most thrilling thing, because sort of erroneously, I thought, yes, I am meant to do this. *Frasier* came from the *Cheers* legacy, and he was one of my favorite characters. So, that's a series, and it's being done by the same people!? *That* series is going to go. I'm set. I'm done. I'm going to get residuals. It's going to go for five years. It'll go into syndication, and I'll be a success.

The role of Roz came down to me and Peri Gilpin. We both

went to the network [NBC executives for a final casting decision]. And we kind of fell in love with each other; we just really connected. We went out to eat after, and we said, "Well, good luck to you! Good luck to you!" You know. It wasn't a competitive thing at all.

That was the smart part. If I'm going to give myself credit for anything, it's for the training I had around auditioning in the business. Not just acting—but around the fact that this is all a *business*. While it feels very personal, they're making business decisions.

I had this great acting teacher, Ian Tucker, and his whole thing was, "I'm not here to teach you to act, because it doesn't seem to matter, honestly." He would name certain people on TV that he didn't think were very good and say, "That person's working all the time; it doesn't matter. It's more about, can you cope [with being rejected or fired]?"

Actors are always fired. Almost every actor has an "I got fired" story. And in television pilots, people get fired all the time. They recast frequently when something's not working mid-shoot. And then sometimes, after the pilot's shot, they recast and reshoot the pilot. So, you're never safe until you see yourself on the show when it airs.

Anyway, everyone is at the table read for *Frasier*—the director, Jimmy Burrows, the network execs, and the studio. I notice that I'm not getting laughs like I did at the audition. I thought, "Am I nervous? What's going on?" I also broke out in hives before I started reading, and I thought, "*What?* I don't do this. Why is this happening right now? Huh, that's weird."

Then, during rehearsals, I notice that something's not working, and I'm not sure what it is. I'm doing the same thing that I did in the audition. And then Jimmy says, when we're preparing for a run-through that day, "No, everyone's too mean to Frasier. We need Roz to not be mean to him." And I was like, er, that's sort of the whole comedic drive with this character.

So, it just wasn't working. I got called in to talk with the producers, David Angell, Peter Casey, and David Lee. And they said, "During the audition, it was different." And I said, "Well, Jimmy was saying that everyone's too mean and that you'd have to rewrite it." And they just went, "Oh, OK, huh." Like that seemed to be news to them.

Then, God bless me, I said, "But you know what I can do? I'm good at dumb characters; I'm good at playing, like, airhead things. So, I can usually make that funny. I think there's gold to be mined in that." And they said, "OK..."

The next day I got a call. I was fired. "It's just not working. We really wanted it to, you know, and it's not." And I said, "OK, well, that's all right. Thank you."

To me, that's the girl thing: let me make this easy for you, and then I'll just go cope later. But I wasn't mad because they're such decent people. They sent me flowers.

But it was kind of brutal. Realizing, wait, I'm not going to see Jane Leeves anymore, or David Hyde Pierce—because I bonded with them already. I thought, "Oh, weird. I don't have their phone numbers yet. I'm just disappearing."

And even with all that great training, when I got fired, I thought maybe I'm not meant to do this. Maybe I don't have the kind of luck you need to do this. Maybe this just won't work out for me because I had the sure thing, and I couldn't keep it. I couldn't keep this job. Now I'm starting over again.

To agent types, I was a long shot, anyway. It wasn't like, "Hey, you've got something." I don't know if they thought that. And at one point, one of my agents, who was trying to be supportive, said (and this is not untrue), "You know, even for comedy sitcoms, they want, like, *gorgeous*. So, it's hard."

And honestly, I didn't think, "So, I'm ugly." But I did think I had a chance in comedy because it didn't require you to be gorgeous or sexy, you know? Because I knew that I wasn't those things. I mean, I'd gotten guest star roles—it's not like I didn't work at all. But I knew the *career* would be a TV series. That was the shot, and it didn't happen.

I didn't doubt my ability. But I wasn't sure if my ability would translate into being able to support myself. I had just quit my day job, which was, luckily enough, working as a receptionist at my father's office. I'd done a pilot a few years before, *Romy and Michele*, which didn't get picked up, but a pilot pays you for a while. That would cover the rent for like a year or two. [The pilot may not have gotten picked up, but Kudrow went on to star in the hit film *Romy and Michele's High School Reunion*.]

But when I was fired from *Frasier*, I still got paid for the pilot. So, that would be good for, like, a year of rent. I didn't have to worry about health insurance because I was in the actors' union.

I tend to be a long-term thinker. And in that moment, it wasn't like, oh, something else will come up. It was more, what's going to happen?

What Next

I gave a commencement address at Vassar [Kudrow is an alumna with a bachelor of arts in biology] fifteen years ago, and I talked about this because it's good for people heading into the workforce: You get a lot of signs. See them as an opportunity, giving you direction.

After I got fired, I don't know what it was in me, but I got up every morning and took a long walk outside. I would end up at a place, Michel Richard, a French patisserie. I treated myself to coffee and a *pain au chocolat*, every day.

One day I got a phone call from [actor] Richard Kind. I knew him from a guest starring role I did on *Mad About You*, and we became friends. I told him about being fired from *Frasier*. "If it were me," he said, "I wouldn't be able to get out of bed every morning or leave the house. How do you even get up and leave the house?"

I thought, "Oh, I *am* doing those things. So, I must be OK." That was a huge boost. And that kind of flipped a switch in my mindset. It still wasn't easy; there was still stuff to process. But I felt like, "I am OK." Really slowly, second by second, minute by minute, day by day.

I also had nothing to lose. I put myself out there with a man that I re-met at a friend's birthday party. It was two weeks after I got fired, and I was still a little fragile. I'd always had this guy in mind, like, "God, he's so great, but he's out of my league." But we met again, and he said hello. We talked about tennis. I said, "Well, we should play tennis. Here's my number." I never did that . . . ever.

Nothing to lose. He called, and we started dating. He's my husband now. We've been married for thirty years.

But in a few months I was going to need to get a day job. One other thing that was happening, though: because I was taking walks every day, my hair was getting bleached from the sun. I have brown hair, but it gave me gold highlights. So, when I'd get my color done, I'd say, "Can you match those? I'm lightening up."

So, the colorist would match the highlights, and in a slow process, over six months, I became blonder. But I was also lightening up emotionally. When I looked in the mirror, instead of the dark-brown moody girl, there was this lighter person. With an attitude of nothing to lose.

One morning I got a call from my agent, saying, "Danny Jacobson, the showrunner from *Mad About You*, wants you to come back." My guest role had been the year before. This was not the same character, she didn't even have a name: it just said "Waitress." And I had to be there in an hour.

I said, "I'm going to do it." But my agents weren't supportive. They thought the part was too small for me. They said, "Come on, you got cast on the *Frasier* pilot." And I thought, "OK, but I also got fired from it. I'm in no position to say no to this. And this is the best show on TV. How fantastic that I get to come back."

I had no idea what I'd be doing. They were like, "We don't even have a script; we just have sides [condensed scripts], and you won't see them till you get there. You won't even know what you're doing."

I said, "Yeah, that's OK." I got ready, got in the car, and said to myself, "Whatever it is, you listen, respond, and flip the comedy switch. That's all you have to do."

The part *was* really small, just one scene. A few lines. Waiting on set, I liked to just sit and watch Paul Reiser and Helen Hunt, because to me that's learning a lot. After we did my scene, Danny Jacobson joined me and said, "You're very funny. We just think you're so great." And I said, "Thank you." He said, "Would it be OK with you if we had you come back like five more times?"

I didn't know whether to pass out or cry with relief. Just like, "Oh, I can rest now. I don't need a day job yet." It was like getting another shot. And *Mad About You* was the best; there was something filmic about it. Remember, normally you don't get to choose the qualities of the show you're on. That's going to be your job. And I just felt so lucky. The pay was like $5,000 an episode, so that was $30,000. That covered my rent for more than a year, and that was fantastic.

Mad About You aired, and some people thought I was funny as the waitress [the character, Ursula Buffay, became so popular that the creators of *Friends* made Kudrow's character, Phoebe, her twin sister]. Paul Reiser, who's just the nicest, most real human being, called me one morning and said, "Hey, I just did an interview on a radio show; callers were calling in and mentioning that they liked *you*, and thought you were so good. I hope it's OK I'm calling you." I was like, "Of course it's OK!"

One of the writers on *Mad About You* was Jeffrey Cleric [partner of David Crane, who went on to create *Friends* with Marta Kauffman]. I loved the writers. I was in The Groundlings [an improvisational comedy troupe in LA], and a lot of people from the group became comedy writers, and a lot of those writers gave me opportunities. When writers were on set, I'd say hi and get to know them. At the time I thought I had more in common with writers than with actors. They were my friends.

Because of *Mad About You*, I had a lot of opportunities for pilot season. There was a Fox pilot which was at the same time as the *Friends* audition process (well, it was called *Friends Like Us* at the time). *Friends Like Us* wanted me to go to their network, NBC, too.

I thought, "Pilots don't go anywhere. I know everyone loves this *Friends Like Us* pilot, it's good, but I don't know." Nothing gets picked up, and if it does get picked up, maybe you get the first thirteen episodes, and then they don't pick up the back nine. You've done half a season.

But this *Friends Like Us* show is on NBC. And so is *Mad About You*. So, I'm thinking, "I bet I could keep my job at *Mad About You* as a recurring character if I'm on an NBC show. Also, everyone seems to want to be on *this* pilot, which is phenomenal. And yeah, I've gotten this far. I like what I've done with the Phoebe character. I could do that for five years if I have to, you know." (That's always the other thing when you signed, you had to commit to doing the show for five years. Now it's six or seven years.)

David Crane was aware of me through Jeffrey Cleric, and Jeffrey said, "What about her for Phoebe?" because it was a tough role to cast. [In quite the twist, Jimmy Burrows, who fired Kudrow from *Frasier*, was the director of the *Friends* pilot.]

It was a lot of auditions, the process for *Friends*. I went straight to the producers, but I also had to audition for Jimmy Burrows.

Just him. I assumed, "Well, it's a pilot, so I'm sure everybody has to audition for Jimmy." (I didn't find out until 2016—when there was a tribute to Jimmy on NBC, and the six of us were on a stage—that I was the *only one* who auditioned for him.)

Anyway, my radar was like, "I wonder if this is going to be OK. Maybe he doesn't get me... I don't know what it is." So, I had that audition. It was just a quick monologue, the first speech Phoebe makes around the table with Rachel, "Oh God, I know what you're talking about, you know, after my mom killed herself..."

It was just Jimmy and me, across a desk. But thank God my training kicked in. You're just going to do what you do. Don't monitor how you're doing. You get to act for a minute and a half. When I was done, he went, "No notes." And I said, "OK, thank you." I got up and left.

Now, "No notes" could mean, yeah, this girl is beyond help, or could mean, yeah, it's good, I don't have any notes on it. It's ambiguous, but I knew enough not to torture myself over it.

And then it was, "You're moving on." [Kudrow was cast in the pilot.]

In the first week of shooting, there was a moment when we were shooting that little monologue, and we're around the table, and Jimmy said, "Lisa, go under the table."

"What?"

"Sit under the table."

So, I'm sitting under the table, I can't see anyone because they're all... up there. And he's like, "It's funny. Let's try it." And I do it. And he's like, "Yeah, that's funny. Let's do it in the run-through."

And I thought, "Oh my God, I'm getting fired again. I'm physically removed from the rest of the cast." I knew there was already a struggle with the idea of "Why are they friends with *her*? She's so weird."

So, we have the run-through. And sure enough, David Crane, who's so sweet and diplomatic, says, "Um, Lisa, I'm not sure it works that you're under the table." And I'm thinking, "Oh God, he thought that was *my* idea." Now he's talking to an actor who has the worst instincts. There's no doubt they're wondering, "Her? That sensibility? I don't know."

And then Jimmy just went, "No, no, that was my idea. They don't always work. All right. She doesn't have to sit under there." And I just went [heavy sigh], "Thank you."

What I Learned

Could I imagine a world where I didn't get *Friends*? Well, my first love before acting was the sciences. I was a biology major. I was interested in evolutionary biology and the evolution of behavior.

I always thought, "I'll be OK." And I'm sorry to say that part of me was like, "You know, at some point you'll get married, and your husband will, of course, be making more money than you do." Because it was a fact.

[It turned out differently. Years later, in *Friends*' final season, the cast negotiated together for the equal pay of $1 million each per episode.]

Some of us knew when it was time to go, but some of us went, "I don't understand why we are stopping. The longer we're here, the more we get paid and the less we have to do." I agreed with that. And people still liked the show.

Personally, I'm not of the "go out when you're on top" mindset, because there's something ego driven about that. For me, it's go when it's time to go—meaning, when they don't need to see you anymore. And you don't have to wait for the hook; there are signs before that. I also like a schedule!

My greatest learning from being fired from *Frasier*? I knew, ultimately, I would be all right, whether I was doing this or not, but in terms of acting, the most important thing I knew was that I didn't want to do anything else. It clarified that.

I remember speaking with Robin Schiff, who wrote *Romy and Michele*, and she said, "I know it won't feel like this, but please believe me, when one door closes, another door opens. It's just true, if you could just believe that."

I had trouble believing that, but it turned out to be true. Over and over, it turned out to be true. And not just from getting fired, it's from any kind of disappointment, like, "Oh, I thought I was going to get to do that thing, and I didn't." Thank God! Because I wouldn't have been available for that independent film that I loved, and I got to meet that person...

I think we're allowed to choose how we see the world. We frame what the experience is. I'm always so impressed with people who have jobs that a lot of people would complain about—who are just happy. You can be good at whatever it is you're doing, and you can be happy with yourself.

What you have or don't have in life doesn't matter. It's what's happening in your head. Because there are plenty of people, and

I worked with one of them for ten years, who... it didn't fix anything. We all can be happy. It's a choice.

Being fired doesn't define you. And just try to believe, *believe*, that it happened for the best. It's not fun to experience right now, but later on you probably will be able to see, "Oh, good thing that happened." Especially if you can have that mindset as you move through whatever your next phase is. It'll be easier to get the next job if you're open and OK.

And sometimes there's a reason you got fired. You have to check in with that. Is it just because your business can't afford you and tons of people are getting fired, or is it something else?

You need to take care of yourself: If you take a job for a while that is not on your career path, you don't need to let people know, "This isn't who I am." You need to let everybody know, "I'm doing the best job anyone's done in this position. *That's* who I am."

As for me, I've held on to a lot of my training. I also know that I'm incredibly fortunate. Really fortunate. I don't have to work. To do something now, I need to really know why I'm doing it. I have to be very clear on that. And that's a privilege.

But... maybe that is for everybody. If it's something that goes against your core principles, maybe you can't take that job. And if you get fired, it's OK to have some despair. But don't allow it for too long. At some point you've got to start looking on the bright side.

3

Do You Need a Lawyer?

Knowing Your Rights and When to Call In the Experts

L egal help isn't just for courtroom dramas—it's about clarity, fairness, and ensuring you leave the situation with your rights and dignity intact. When we got canned, we both called employment lawyers. And nope, this was not someone we had on speed dial. Instead, we had to hurriedly ask around for recommendations. But remember, every industry has a grapevine: just ask enough people and you'll get good intel. (There is also, of course, the internet, but it's overwhelming steering through all those sponsored lawyer posts: finding a lawyer who's worked with someone you know is a shorthand you'll be grateful for.)

While it feels particularly awful to prolong an already shitty situation, bringing in a legal expert to review your options is one of the smartest moves you can make. (Sidenote: if you're in a union, call your representative and ask if you can talk to someone on their legal team.) While we were feeling like beetles on our backs, talking to someone whose entire mission is to protect your rights in the workplace was a game changer. In Kristina's case, her lawyer had worked with the company before, so he had useful insight into how they operated.

For context again, we were both in senior roles—Laura had an employment contract and Kristina had terms that were negotiated when she signed her offer letter a decade before. But no matter your level, consulting a lawyer may be more helpful (and affordable) than you think.

Whether you're thinking about suing the bastards, pushing for more severance, or just reviewing the terms to make sure you're not getting screwed, knowing that you maturely explored your options gives you power. (Maturity is the goal here—this is not to imply your authors have achieved it, but smart choices do feel good.)

When hiring a lawyer, it's crucial to find someone who not only has strong legal expertise but also understands the nuances of your specific industry. Laws and regulations can vary wildly between professional fields and locations—whether it's media, tech, retail, finance, or government jobs—so working with a lawyer who speaks your industry's language means they can navigate complex issues and provide targeted advice. Go with someone who has a proven track record—put those trusty recs to work—and find someone who has secured a good outcome for someone you know. All of which can save you time, money, and headaches in the long run. (The best part: they handle the dirty work and will be the one to make the awkward calls with your ex-bosses, not you.)

How Much Is a Lawyer, Anyway?

Hiring a lawyer sounds intimidating and expensive, and you likely may not have had to deal with one over the course of your career. In the United States, the national average is between $200 and $400 an hour, but it gets *much* higher ($500 to $1,200-ish an hour) in New York, DC, and Los Angeles.* The good news is that in employment cases, the financial burden will likely not fall entirely on you.

The magic word? Contingency. "A lot of lawyers take employment cases on contingency," labor attorney Shannon Liss-Riordan says. "We barely have any clients who pay out of pocket, and those who do don't pay up front. We take their cases on contingency so that we only get paid if we win or reach a resolution for their case."

Liss-Riordan continues, "The law recognizes that working people don't have the funds to pay for lawyers the way corporations do. So, reach out to a lawyer if you've been terminated (or think you're about to be terminated) to understand your rights—without concern that you can't pay.

"There are also a lot of plaintiff's lawyers who require some retainer [a fee paid up front] to talk. So, depending on who you're

---

* No surprises here but things really do vary wildly according to where you live! Our advice is to reach out to a handful of reputable professionals in order to get a better understanding of the going rate in your location.

trying to speak to, you may have to pay something. But you can also keep looking. And if you have a real case, there will be a lawyer who will talk to you without charging you up front."

Organizations like the Legal Aid Society, or its international equivalents, provide legal expertise to low-income people. Your city or state bar association will also have referrals to lawyers working pro bono, meaning the fees or commissions are much lower than a regular lawyer or none at all.

If you're not in a position to hire a lawyer with a capital *L*, HR and talent expert Bucky Keady suggests, "Reach out to someone you might know who's in law school. Look into free legal services. Some companies also have an EAP [Employee Assistance Program] that you can call and get free legal advice."

And don't be afraid to fire up ChatGPT for assistance. It can be a valuable tool for breaking down the complex legalese often found in severance agreements. It can also niftily summarize public information on standard severance packages, so you can better understand the landscape. At the very least, it can help you craft a baseline "what to ask for" script for meeting with a lawyer or negotiating directly with your former employer.

If You Know Layoffs Are Coming, Call a Lawyer

Your company was just acquired? Merged? Announced a new AI platform? Went bankrupt? Buyouts brewing? Whatever's going on, you're reading the room, and it's not looking good? Well, if you have your wits about you, calling a lawyer *before* anything happens is a great strategy. Then you're able to arm yourself with knowledge of any possible recourse before you're asked to take a seat at that giant, lonely conference table in the HR department.

Liss-Riordan says, "An employee may have legal rights or potential claims that they're not aware of. I advise people to try to speak to a lawyer if they think a termination is coming. There are various ways that terminations can be illegal. For example, if they're the result of discrimination or retaliation." Most of the time, there's not a legal right at stake, but "If there is an issue in the workplace—wage related, discrimination, or harassment—if you assert your rights before you're terminated, it's possible that you may be protected. This may give the employer second thoughts about taking action against you. And then if you do get terminated, you may potentially have a claim for retaliation. A lawyer can give you advice about things you can do to put yourself in a better position even before the termination happens."

Also, it's helpful to research what the severance package policies are where you live, as they differ between industries and all over the world. "Severance packages can be negotiable," says executive recruiter Kristy Hurt. "Unfortunately, many states do not require any severance at all. So, depending on what state you're in, you should understand what the legal requirements are. Because if a company goes out of business and everyone gets fired and no one gets severance, often there's no recourse."

So...look it up. Employment discrimination litigator Jennifer Liu gives an example: "In California, when you are terminated, the employer has to give you all pay that you are due, and it has to be on that day of termination. If you are not paid all your wages due, then you get a full day of pay for *every day* they are late. The company drags its feet up to a cap of thirty days. That can really add up: I once got somebody like twenty thousand dollars because their company messed up."

Yes, Getting Fired Sucks—But Is It Illegal?

After you are shown the door, a lawyer can be of major assistance by, one, helping you navigate this wildly stressful period, and two, determining if you have a case for wrongful termination (a.k.a. you were fired illegally). Title VII, which prohibits employment discrimination based on certain characteristics, and other employment laws are complex, and it's smartest to let the pros figure out if your firing crossed a legal line. A lawyer can also help you navigate the Equal Employment Opportunity Commission (EEOC), where you must file a complaint *before* you sue your employer.

So, yes—you're upset, offended, freaked out about money, but is there legitimate wrongdoing on your employer's part? "Unfortunately, there's nothing illegal about just being fired in a way you think is unfair," says Liss-Riordan. "If there is something illegal about it [a case of discrimination, for example], it's not necessarily something that a layperson will know the answer to unless they consult with a lawyer. Also, a lot of people have to just make their own decision about whether they want to pursue something or just move on with their life."

If the firing is illegal and unjust, you have a chance not just to win your case, but to help others further down the road. "Litigated court rulings create precedent that help develop, establish, and enforce laws. It's important for employees and the system as a whole for people to stand up for their rights, take these cases to court, and force companies to live up to their obligations."

Also, a good lawyer should be able to tell you in a timely way if you have a case, rather than stringing you along, charging for more hours. "It's of huge value to tell people that they *don't* have a legal case," says Elizabeth Saylor, citywide director of the Employment Law Unit at the Legal Aid Society. "A lot of people think it's illegal if your boss wrongly fired you because he said you were late and you weren't late, he accused you of doing something that you didn't do, or he yelled at you all the time."

And while that's undeniably awful, "It's usually not illegal, unless the boss did it because of a protected category—race, gender, etc.—or retaliated against you for certain complaints. Or perhaps because you're engaging in union activity or you're reporting a health concern or something like that. [But] we live in a country where, with some exceptions, you don't need a good cause to fire someone."

"Sometimes reasons for termination can be extremely unfair," adds Liu. "They can be inflammatory or arbitrary, but unless they're illegal or the way that the person is fired is illegal, it's not legally actionable." There is some nuance, however: "If, say, your boss believes that you're not very good at your job (because your boss is a misogynist and doesn't think that women in general are very good at their jobs), then maybe that is an illegal reason. It can look very similar but may not rise to the level of a legal claim."

What Is an Illegal Firing?

Jennifer Liu gave us the rundown on what constitutes an illegal firing:

Breach of Contract

"In more traditional industries or higher-level positions, people often have an employment agreement. If they are terminated and not given all the things that they are owed, that is a breach of contract."

Discrimination

"Usually when it's discrimination, the employer, manager, or the decision-maker at the company doesn't even think it was a discriminatory decision."

Educate yourself about what's referred to as "protective class" (workplace protection due to race, gender, disability, sexual orientation, religion, pregnancy, etc.), to see if you may fit under that umbrella. "The employer may think the [protective class] person was just not as good or broke a rule, but when you compare what they actually did to a person who was *not* in a protective class, you can see very different treatments."

Retaliation

"Retaliation is the most common claim we see because usually when there is discrimination, you also see retaliation. For example, if somebody complains, 'I think my manager is not treating me as seriously or giving me these opportunities because I'm a woman—he seems to be giving all the opportunities to men and goes out to lunch with them.' Maybe that woman makes a complaint or raises something to HR.

"What often happens is when people complain about discrimination, companies resent it or the decision-maker finds out about it, or simply the employer starts to not trust the person as much and thinks they might be trying to set the company up for a claim. But often I see employees who are just trying to be heard and helped, and the company starts to manage itself in a liability-oriented way. People hold grudges; it's human nature."

Whistleblowers

"Perhaps somebody raises a health and safety concern about what's going on in their company or financial improprieties; problems with the financial statements or the auditing. Often when people are whistleblowers, it doesn't end well because the company recognizes them as a threat and wants to manage them out."

So, Should You Bring a Case?

Spend some time closely reviewing your odds of winning. A lawyer will help you determine if you even *want* to bring a case against your employer. Saylor says, "While I think everyone should contact a lawyer if they can, I don't think everyone should bring a lawsuit."

For example, what if you have a case, but you're up against a company with murky financials? "A huge problem for our clients here at Legal Aid is they work for small businesses or businesses that are good at hiding their assets," says Saylor. "Even if the person is owed a huge amount of money, it doesn't make sense to sue your employer if you're going to get a judgment that you can never collect on.

"If you work for a financial firm or a big company," she adds, "it's a lot easier to collect, but a lot of companies—restaurants, trucking companies, construction companies—are hard to pin down. So, if you sue them and get a judgment, you might not be able to collect. We have a lot of cases we can't collect on. Like a nail salon case, we had a judgment of $600,000 that we got ten years ago at a trial. We collected only a small amount of it."

Well, that's depressing. But it's smart to think about if you want to spend your time and emotional well-being on something that, however unfairly, may not reward you in the end. A lawyer helps move you off an emotional plane to a more practical one, offering odds and perspective that can sometimes get lost. "Employment cases also are often very emotional," says Saylor. "To have a lawyer look at the facts, find out your goals, and work through that can be very helpful because it's not always in your best interest."

Even if you have a good claim, the odds might stack against you "if you're young or you're in an insular job industry. While it is 100 percent illegal to retaliate against someone for asserting their rights, it's a piece of paper, and the law is not always easy to enforce."

What You Don't Want: Arbitration

"Arbitration is a form of alternative dispute resolution (ADR)," says Liu. And it most often benefits the employer because, guess what, the employers hire the arbitrator.

Arbitration is a way to resolve a dispute without going to court.

"What the parties are doing is agreeing to go to a neutral third party," explains Liu. "The arbitrator will preside over the 'discovery' phase of the case (where both sides exchange information to preview the claims).

"Then the arbitrator will hold the hearing, which is like a mini trial. If it happens in person, the arbitrator sits in a conference room. Each side, usually with attorneys, will present their witnesses and their documentary evidence. But instead of having a jury listen, the arbitrator decides and issues the decision, usually in writing."

Arbitration is often seen as a faster way to resolve disputes. There is generally less discovery than is done in court, which of course keeps costs down.

But here's where it gets tricky for the employee: "Once you get the arbitrator's decision, it's basically final. There is the right to appeal like there is in court. From the employee's perspective, arbitration is horrible. It deprives employees of their right to get information that's relevant to their claims in the name of saving the corporation's money."

And remember, the arbitrators don't work for you; they work for your employer. "Arbitrators all work for private arbitration companies. In employment cases, they get paid by the employer. So, what ends up happening is there is a tendency for arbitrators to favor employers in disputes because employers are repeat players and employees are not," says Liu.

"There is a tendency for arbitration decisions to come down in favor of employers more [so] than in the court system. There's also a tendency that even when the employee wins, the awards are much, much lower than people get from juries in court. It really stands in the way of a lot of more vulnerable people, whether they be people of color or women or people who might have some kind of medical condition or disability that has forced them out of their job, and they don't get the same ability to get justice because of an arbitration agreement."

Where a Lawyer Can Really Help: Severance

As we said earlier, there is absolutely no harm in asking for more severance or arguing that you're entitled to it. Negotiating money is a less emotional transaction than litigating workplace behavior. So, if you think you can get a bigger payout, go for it.

An employment lawyer can also act like a corporate Cyrano de Bergerac, helping you craft your arguments for greater compensation in the background. "The other side is more likely to listen and negotiate if you have a lawyer," says Saylor. "But sometimes it is good for the lawyer to be behind the scenes; we will advise people on their severance agreement or their negotiations, draft emails for them, or do other things without making ourselves known."

Like so many things in life, it's a matter of reading the room: Are you better placed to make a "direct" emotional plea (with some legal coaching) to a sympathetic employer? Would sending an aggressive lawyer straight to the front lines antagonize the people you are negotiating with, so they give you the proverbial finger? Based on all of those relationships, make a battle plan and decide if you want your lawyer behind the scenes or out in front.

Either way, remember, when you are given an agreement to

sign upon termination, you are under no obligation to sign it right away. Send it to your lawyer or take time to review it yourself in detail. (If you're over forty, you are protected under the Older Workers Benefit Protection Act. Your employer must give you twenty-one days to review the agreement if you're the only one being let go and forty-five days to review if you're part of a group layoff. And most important: you have seven days to revoke your acceptance, even after signing.)

If you don't understand something, find someone with contract or legal experience who can help define terms you may be confused about. "Many people, when they're let go, are given some kind of separation agreement to sign. Especially at bigger companies," says Liu. "They are often pretty standard, but that doesn't mean that they can't be negotiated in some way. They could be made more balanced and more protective of the employee. But separation agreements are created to protect the employer and that's why they're usually tough to amend."

Are You Owed Wages?

If you're owed money, get your money! Often you'll have a better shot with this than by disputing the termination itself. An employment lawyer can help you determine if you're owed wages you might have no idea about. "Wage law is very complicated and confusing, and if you're not trained in employment law, you would have no idea that you had some right that was being violated," says Liss-Riordan. She says people most often call simply because they're upset about being terminated, then realize later they may be owed money. Remember, severance is not typically required by law, unless it's part of a contract, so it's good to have someone else thinking strategically for you.

"The lawyer might tell them that, unfortunately, they can't do anything legally about their termination, but it turns out that they were misclassified as overtime exempt for years and they're owed a lot of money. Or they're misclassified as independent contractors and they're owed money, or there's some other legal violation that they weren't aware of. You may be leaving money on the table because you've got rights that you aren't aware of."

What you have better odds of claiming: health care. Liu says, "[Employers] usually have to give the employee a COBRA [the Consolidated Omnibus Budget Reconciliation Act, which temporarily maintains health insurance] notice so that the employee has information about continuing their health-care coverage if they're receiving health-care coverage through the employer."

Is There a Case for Class Action?

If there are many people in the company who have been affected like you, you may be able to band together with other laid-off employees and file a class-action lawsuit. You have the power of a group to rely on and won't have to shoulder a legal bill on your own. So, if you have a case, pursue it.

"The most typical type of class action is a wage dispute where the same issue affects a lot of people," explains Liss-Riordan. "Some of the most common are overtime misclassification.

"There may be some wage issue where the company was paying everyone the wrong way, they didn't pay a bonus the way they promised, they weren't calculating wages correctly, or they were docking for breaks when people weren't able to take them."

Liss-Riordan says discrimination can be a cause for a class-action suit, too. "Sometimes there are discrimination claims that can be pursued if there is a protected category of people who are being discriminated against in a similar way, like women or racial minorities or other protected classes."

She brings up a case she may be working on for the next millennium: "I'm suing Twitter, now X, for a lot of broken promises. When Elon Musk bought the company in 2022, the employees had been promised very generous severance in the event of layoffs after he took over. When he came in, he just ignored those promises. So, we have about a dozen class-action lawsuits in courts related to those layoffs, as well as two thousand individual arbitrations because the company tried to block class actions from going forward and compelled the employees to arbitration."

While none of these situations are fun, if you can band together, you have a team behind you, which (hopefully) lessens the pain.

Put Your Union to Work

Employment disputes are what unions are for! If you're a member of one, use it. Liss-Riordan has some pointers:

"If you're in a unionized workplace, there are additional rights that you may have. And if you think the employer is doing something that is against the rules or just not right, reach out to the union. They may be able to provide some assistance, either advice behind the scenes or having someone with you when you're having a discussion with management or HR."

Perhaps a union can help you get ahead of things. "If it's something the union can raise with the company *before* the termination happens, they may get involved in that. And if there are a number of people who are experiencing the same issue, it's something that a union may help with." Remember, it's all considered part of your membership.

If You Don't Hire a Lawyer...

Try to do the following four things so you have the best chance at resolving your dispute:

At Least Consult a Lawyer (They Won't Charge for the First Call)

Talk to a lawyer before you shoot off your mouth to your former employer. "Sometimes we see people who've already done and said things that undermine their case," says Liu. "We might think, this is a really strong case, and we could get this person one or two years of their pay. But at some point, they say, 'It's three months or nothing,' or 'I won't send an agreement!' If someone's already started a negotiation and indicated they're willing to settle for much less than what their claim is worth, they will make it much harder to get to where they want to go. They didn't understand some of the usual dance moves that people make in negotiations."

Don't Sign Anything Right Away

We've said this like three times now—but do not! Liss-Riordan concurs. "It's not uncommon for employers to give you a severance package with a very short deadline to sign it. Usually, you can negotiate to get more time, especially if you're trying to talk to a lawyer about it.

"We recommend people talk to a lawyer and request that the deadline be pushed back. The company will usually keep that offer open beyond the deadline, especially if someone has counsel." So, don't freak out about the ticking clock. "It's usually negotiable to give them a little more time to think about their options. If they don't know the reason they were terminated, if it hasn't been spelled out, we advise people just to simply ask what the reason is.

"It might be best to just put that in an email so that you have a written record. Employers won't respond, but it doesn't hurt to ask. And even the fact that you asked, and they didn't respond, could be telling. So, if there's an exit interview or an opportunity to talk with the employer, it behooves employees to listen more than to speak because they might learn something."

It's like any good interview: let the subject reveal their intentions without dominating the conversation. You can, of course, have your say to your employer—hell, this is *your* exit—but the real power in this interaction comes from listening.

Know Your Rights, Especially in Mass Layoffs

There are rules regarding mass layoffs—when a company fires 33 percent or more of its workforce—and how much notice employees need to receive. "Generally speaking, under the Federal WARN (Worker Adjustment and Retraining Notification) Act, employers who engage in mass layoffs have to provide sixty days advance notice of the layoff or sixty days of pay in lieu of notice. The point is to provide a transition period for people, to help them find their next position." This applies globally too, though different countries will have different legal requirements. Check what rules apply to your company and region.

Archive and Back Up Your Emails and Documents

Were you subjected to months of inappropriate emails or texts from your boss? Is there evidence of illegal goings-on in your inbox? Or even a guaranteed raise by a certain date that never materialized? "Get your documents together and figure out what you have," recommends Saylor. "Do you have emails? If they weren't paying more hours, had you kept track of that? Think about your goal and who could back you up."

Of course, hindsight is 20/20, and ideally you'd be collecting these documents *before* you get the boot. It's unlikely you'll have access to your inbox for very long—it might be only a matter of hours—after you've been laid off.

Either way, as Laura is fond of saying, "Cover your ass in paper pants."

4

Tracy Sherrod

Tracy Sherrod is a book publishing vice president and executive editor. She was laid off from Little, Brown in 2024.

"My job did not give me strength. It did not give me identity. It did not give me the things that my life support system did."

What Happened

We could tell the layoffs were coming. The publisher and CEO were let go in March, so changes would be made. We were all just waiting: When is this announcement going to happen?

My most immediate concern was money, finances. So, the minute I thought there might be layoffs, I started tightening up everything—paying off any outstanding credit card balances, all of those things, so I would have a clean slate if I lost my job.

Then one morning the editorial team got a series of these meeting invites. So, we're all texting back and forth, saying, "Keep it cool," trying to be one another's moral support. Telling each other, "Don't cry, don't lose your grace."

Seven of us were let go. The layoffs happened one by one, and then we called each other afterward to commiserate. All of the junior editors (who were paid less) stayed. It was nice that they kept them.

We didn't know who else was being let go outside of the editorial group. Then I started getting farewell emails from various colleagues. An art director sent me a beautiful note about how the books I published had really allowed him to show range in his department and that he would miss working with me. I read it and said, "Oh my God, you know they let me go, too!" And he was like, "Now I *know* it's crazy." At some point, people were able to laugh about it.

The same day we were let go, the publisher sent out an industry-wide press release announcing the "restructuring." I tried to do my best to reply to all the people who reached out to me, but I was also focused on finishing up an edit on a book that was important to me. So, I would try to spend just an hour a day sending emails, replying, saying thank you, all that kind of stuff. And while I was busy doing that, I missed an email from someone who had reached out to me about a job!

We were given a few weeks' notice. Once I finished editing that last book, I started to calm down—not having my mind racing or just focused in one area. I made a list of who I needed to get back to. And then there were people reaching out for lunch dates, to let me know there was support for me. That was really thoughtful, but I knew one of the most important things was to try to get some rest.

Then the press picked up the news, including *The New York Times*, which started a thing about "Is diversity working or not in publishing?" It was in *The Atlantic* as well. It keeps popping up. They reached out to me for interviews and comments, but that's not what I wanted to do. I just wanted to relax my mind, and so I didn't reply to any of the media requests.

What Next

I remember being a young editor in the '90s and walking past the office of a friend who was an executive editor. He was distracted and acting a bit off. When I asked him what was the matter, he said, "I think I'm going to get fired."

"What are you talking about?" I said. "You just won the Pulitzer. One of your authors just won the Pulitzer Prize. No *way* would you get fired!"

He was let go a few weeks later. It blew my mind. That's how naive I was. But it began to plant the seed that, you know, "What have you done for me lately?" means something. It also means higher-ups want different things.

I never think of firings as personal. Especially when it's at a certain level in your career. As a wise person in publishing once told me, it usually just comes down to money. They have to cut some salaries, make some margins.

On the upside, think about it: you rarely get moments in life in which you can regroup. In which you can just focus on yourself, focus on your home, focus on your partner and your friendships and all. Just focus and get everything rejiggered.

My husband encouraged me to teach a course on the editorial process at the NYU School for Professional Studies. It was interesting, because it was Monday through Friday, from nine to five. It offered structure, which I hadn't had since I was laid off.

After a few weeks, I started slowly taking those publishing lunches, but only like three a month. They were all enjoyable, but probably not necessarily what I needed at the time. It can take you there emotionally again. Or to emotions I should have had.

[Money-wise] I've been doing a little bit of freelance editing, too, working with different publishers on projects I like. But mostly I'm enjoying the time and the peace of mind.

When the book I finished editing in those final weeks comes out, I'll be really proud. And I do think, if at some point I decide to go back in-house as an editor, I'll cross paths with some of those authors again.

What I Learned

I think that, deep down, the reality is we should all prepare for getting laid off. A corporation is a corporation. It's not your mate. It doesn't determine your identity. It doesn't determine your life fully, and we can't keep allowing it to, even though it's been given personhood by the government. We cannot join ranks with that, or we'll get our minds twisted and our hearts broken.

If you feel it's time to go, you should probably look for a new job—not wait it out. I didn't start looking for something when the new publisher came in because I knew I needed to take a break before I moved on to the next thing.

I've been an editor since 1987. This is the first real break I've had. I stopped at one point to start a literary agency, but that wasn't a break. That was a lot of work.

What I've learned the most, what's changed me the most, is being centered enough to know what *I* want to be doing at all times. I'm an editor. I'm always thinking of book ideas. I'm always thinking of books and words. And most importantly, what I'm going to read next. And to be able to sit and think while reading.

How did getting fired make me stronger? I was already strong. My job did not give me strength. It did not give me identity. It did not give me the things that my life support system did. It was a wonderful place for me to showcase my skills. If I ever get down, I can go to the bookstore, and I can see all those wonderful books that I've worked on. I've made contributions to the world. That's all the satisfaction I need.

I don't care that some people may look at being let go as a bad thing. "Oh, look what happened to her." I don't. It means the universe is saying, either it's time to do what you do someplace else, or it's time to do something else.

Keep your eyes open, and your heart open, and your hands open, so things can come to you, and you can receive them. And just look for good things.

I think we all have fantasies when we're at our jobs, like, what else would we like to do? I've always wanted to teach at one of the Andre Agassi Foundation for Education college prep charter schools for a year. I would go and work at a tennis center. I would love a job in the tennis world. Maybe the USTA [United States Tennis Association] needs someone to help with their publications. I'm going to explore some things, write a letter to Andre.

I'm still thinking about whether I want to go back to a traditional publishing job. That said, I will always believe in the books I've published. One of them was called *Permission to Dream*. I spent a lot of time while I was working on that book just letting my mind dream of what I would do, where I would want to go. I have a lot of dreams, still.

Katie Couric

Katie Couric is the founder of Katie Couric Media. She left the *Today* show to host *CBS Evening News* in 2006. She departed CBS in 2011 when her contract wasn't renewed.

> "If you put too much stock in what a job brings to you and what holes it fills up in you, you're going to be lost."

What Happened

It's hard not to have setbacks, particularly in the media. The whole industry is imploding and transforming in ways we never anticipated would come this quickly. I've had disappointments, but I have also gotten something out of them, as Pollyannaish as that might sound. In the larger landscape of my public TV role, I did fail at CBS on some level. They expected me to be a one-woman savior and change the trajectory of the evening news in a way that, frankly, was unrealistic. [Chairman and CEO] Les Moonves wanted me to reimagine the format and make it more accessible, which the audience didn't want. I was up for the task, but maybe I wasn't right for the job.

It was difficult because CBS hired me for who I was [a polished but unpretentious face viewers had shared their mornings with for years on the *Today* show], but when I showed up being who I was, they didn't really want that in an evening news format. It was also an organizational issue where Les Moonves had a vision that wasn't necessarily shared with the rest of the organization. That really was the problem. Change is very disruptive. In retrospect, I probably shouldn't have taken the job knowing this new iteration of an evening newscast probably wouldn't have worked.

I was the first woman to solo anchor a national evening news program. That was shocking enough for an audience, and then to try to make it feel more relaxed, less buttoned up—that was a bridge too far, honestly. I had this attitude of, I'm just going to try it. Let's see what happens. What's the worst that could happen? But that approach is too theoretical: If you are going into a new role you're not certain about, you need to play it out and say if this doesn't work, what will that mean? How will I feel? What will I do?

In TV news, everything is judged by ratings. The newscast started with a big bang because of the curiosity factor audiences had, but as soon as the ratings started to decline, that was a convenient way of saying this isn't going to work. She's not good. She's not right for this job. So, I think I started to read the room early on. It was palpable. Some people were great and supportive, but you could tell others were suspicious. I understand that; when you have somebody new coming in and upending the organization, that makes people very insecure. I had brought some people over with me, so the people who were already there didn't know whether they would get fired. I get it, but it was still very hard.

I'm surprised I didn't quit before my contract was up. But it wasn't like me to just throw my hands up and leave. I thought that would be shitty for women and just not the right decision. Rick Kaplan, the new executive producer, really saved my bacon by giving me back my confidence and telling me I was the best anchor he had ever worked with. I don't think that's true, but that's what he said—and it made me feel better. So, I'm glad I hung in there. I'm proud of the work I did. I did a pretty consequential interview with Sarah Palin two years in, so I feel like, yeah, I did great work. I showed my worth.

I used to say in speeches, "When you're a trailblazer, you often get burned." The inordinate amount of attention given to how I was going to perform in this role was overwhelming and pretty shocking. It was hard to do a "soft opening." I was the first woman to solo anchor an evening newscast, and it was history making. It was hard to do that under the radar. I think about the women who are the first or even the second or third; how much more pressure is on them, how much more difficult the role can be.

I've always felt that to get a job, you need to have a job, which is kind of old-fashioned thinking. So, when the writing was on the wall, and it was clear [former CBS chairman] Jeff Fager just wasn't that into me and was warming the seat for Scott Pelley—who he worked with at *60 Minutes*—I thought, "What am I going to do next?" Subconsciously I was thinking, "If I have somewhere to go, it won't look like that was such a failure." So, I started identifying and formulating my exit six months or so before my contract was up. I wanted people to know I was moving on, too. Where the fact of the matter is they were moving on from me.

So much of my identity was tied up in the fact that I was an on-air TV journalist-slash-personality-slash-anchor. Especially if it's public—but even if it's not—if you love your job, and you're committed to it, so much of your identity is attached to that. It's really hard.

I was proud of the work I had done. I could point to tangible things I felt good about. And it was clear to me there was internal sexism to a certain degree and external sexism, too. Maybe I just rationalized it in my own mind for self-preservation, but I didn't worry too much about my reputation. I think it's because the job did not necessarily highlight my talents or skills. People gravitate to me because of my authenticity (which is now such an overused word), but also because I'm the same person on and off camera. So, doing the evening news felt a little bit like a straitjacket for me. It wasn't the best fit.

What Next

Having said that, I think doing a syndicated talk show [*Katie*, which aired from 2012 to 2014] was probably a massive overcorrection. I had it in my head that I could do important, serious stories at two or three o'clock in the afternoon, but honestly, that's not what the audience is tuning in for. They're tuning in for entertainment.

I've spent my whole career trying to prove myself as a serious journalist, so to be suddenly doing *Redbook*'s Hottest Husbands or coming in on a plastic horse with bales of hay... I was like, "No, no, no, I'm not doing that." I'm not putting it down; it just wasn't right for me. So, that ended after two years. Once again, I was like, OK, *waah waah*, that didn't work either. I'm used to pivoting and reassessing where I am and where I'm going and in the current job market, everyone needs to become good at that.

I had done every big, important job in network news. So, once you've been to the mountaintop, it's hard to take a job that's of lesser importance—maybe from an ego perspective, maybe just from how challenging it is. I would have loved to have been on *60 Minutes*, and I think I could have lived out the rest of my career at a show like that, which I respect so much.

But I always want to be smart about adjusting to changes and going where the puck is going. And I saw so many people hanging on to legacy media when it really had lost its cultural significance. With Katie Couric Media [a digital news network headlined by Couric, who frequently uses Instagram Live to break news; KCM also features entertainment, lifestyle, health, and shopping content], I thought there is so much more freedom, creativity, and new challenges in becoming an entrepreneur. That was something that I hadn't done yet. That sounded exciting. I was in an enviable position of having established myself as a trusted figure, and I was in the media when it was possible to become a household name. It's increasingly difficult now that everyone's a journalist, everyone's a reporter. So, I thought, why not capitalize on the fact that I have done this, and my personal brand is powerful as well. That was what motivated me.

For all the moaning and groaning about digital media, social media, and the ill effects of it, it has opened so many possibilities. Podcasts weren't around when we started out in the business. There are so many avenues to reach an audience now. If that hadn't existed, and I had come to the end of the road professionally when I turned sixty, I probably would be out of the business altogether. I might have tried to run a nonprofit or done something totally different. But because these options are open to me, I can continue doing what I love to do: talking to people, telling stories, and helping people understand this crazy, complicated world we find ourselves in.

There are so many commercial considerations when you want to address an important topic. And now I talk about whatever I want to talk about. I'm lucky because when I ask for an interview, people know I'll be prepared, that I know what I'm doing, and that I'll do it in a professional, respectful way. I have the best of both worlds, helping me continue to work and stay engaged with the world. Our iPhones have turned into our television sets. I'm not watching much TV news, because we're all on the go. And when I do, it's usually clips that have been cut for social media. You must be open to doing new, interesting, fun things.

What I Learned

The world is changing so quickly, and every industry is going through a massive transformation. So, if you get fired, don't take it personally. There's no shame in having a job that doesn't work out for whatever reason. You took a risk. You tried something, and it didn't work. Next!

I was someone who attached my value to my job. I really went through a difficult time when I was in my early sixties, figuring out who I was. Was I worthy if I wasn't on television every day? What did people think of me? I remember thinking throughout all my jobs in network news—especially on the *Today* show when there was a white-hot spotlight shining on me—that people liked me because of the job I had and what they thought I could do for them. It's a cynical view, but it made me realize that your job isn't you; it isn't who you are. If you know that, and the people around you know that, you'll be fine.

If you put too much stock in what a job brings to you and what holes it fills up in you, you're going to be lost. You need to fill those holes yourself with the things that really matter, appreciate your skills and strengths.

That said, I think a lot of us feel like that. But does the sign with your title on your office door or cubicle say who you are as a person, what makes you happy, what you love? Or is it some label that gives you a certain modicum of status in the world? It's also a cautionary tale: if you invest everything in your job, to the detriment of being a well-rounded person with good friends and passions outside your work, you're screwed. Jobs come and go. You need to be flexible and adaptable, and see where your skills might fit another role. You also need to be a lifelong learner: What are people doing now, and can I do that, too?

I think curiosity is half the equation for me. A desire to share what I know is the second part. I took Myers-Briggs personality tests when I was in high school, and the results all said I should be a social worker. I think that part of me sees my role—and maybe this sounds pretentious—as a bit of a public servant. I love journalism. I love telling stories, but more importantly, I love sharing those stories to make people's lives better.

What would I say to the younger me, who might have been afraid she'd be fired or need to go in a different direction? I would say that, despite it all, and no matter how appealing it might be: don't play it safe.

Health Care

Health-Care Hacks and Finding the Best Coverage for You

Living in the United States affords you many blessings; health care, however, is not one of them. (Dear reader, if you are based outside of the United States, feel free to skip this chapter. Or, you can read it and feel immeasurably better about your homeland's healthcare benefits—and your life in general.) Only in the US does losing your job often also mean losing your ability to afford to see a doctor or get treatment. It's ridiculous, and scary as hell. When we were laid off, we were offered extended medical benefits under our company's insurance plans. In conjunction with COBRA—again, the Consolidated Omnibus Budget Reconciliation Act (catchy!)—your employer can subsidize some of your coverage for a period, depending on the terms of your severance agreement.

According to the U.S. Department of Labor, COBRA requires employers with twenty or more employees to offer a temporary extension of health coverage to employees and their families after their regular coverage ends. This "continuation coverage" gives them the option to keep their health insurance for a while longer, even after losing their job. More on COBRA later.

The health insurance system overall is impossible to navigate: the wildest thing was that Laura's COBRA coverage (which she had for six months) did not kick in until a card arrived *in the mail*. (You know, like the 1950s.) So, for a full week, neither Laura nor her husband had health-care coverage. During these seven days she felt extremely vulnerable (and barely left the house lest she get hit by a bus). Now, because she works for herself, Laura pays almost $2,000 a month to insure herself and the hubs. The dream!

Negotiating extended health-care coverage was just as critical to Kristina as securing her compensation package. With her partner and two children on her plan, losing health care would affect the entire family. Luckily, her company continued to pay for her health care in conjunction with COBRA, which was a crucial bridge, allowing them to stay insured while they sorted their options. It also spared them all running around in a medical frenzy trying to get into every doctor, dentist, gynecologist, and dermatologist in, like, a month.

Both of us, apart from navigating our own situations, also

spent endless time wondering, how on earth do people with fewer resources (or no health insurance in the first place) ever manage? How is it *acceptable* that in the United States, when you lose your job, losing your health care is one of your most urgent fears? And, frankly, why should anyone have to take a job in the first place just because it offers health care? It's not right.

But, given we are stuck with this Godforsaken system, how do you stack the deck to take care of your health, the most important thing of all, after you've been fired?

We asked key experts about what calls to make, when to make them, and what plan to choose, depending on your personal needs and, of course, your income. It's like going shopping—but not in a fun way. This is the information we wished we had.

When You Are Laid Off, Act Right Away

If you lose your job, you will likely lose your company-sponsored health care soon. Some companies cut it off at the end of the month, and if you got laid off, say, on the twenty-ninth, that day could be tomorrow. So, while you might be whimpering under your duvet, throw the covers off for just a minute to make some quick decisions.

"You have zero time to coast," says Caitlin Donovan, senior director of the Patient Advocate Foundation. "The first thing you should do is ask your company's HR people exactly what type of coverage you have and how long you'll have it. For some people, it may go through the end of the month. Some people may transition immediately to COBRA." Most importantly, "Get it in writing."

Before Your Insurance Runs Out, Do This

Go on a Doctor Tour

Wedge in all your annuals, checkups, OB-GYN visits, eye appointments, and dental cleanings while your company is still partially paying for them. You'll feel great that you got it all done, even if all the scheduling and hauling around is stressful. Donovan advises, "Get all of your prescriptions refilled. Go on a health-care spending spree. Now is the time."

Use Your FSA or HSA Funds

An FSA (Flexible Spending Account) or an HSA (Health Savings Account) are employee benefits that let you put aside money on a pre-tax basis to pay for qualified medical expenses. FSAs are tied to your employer, but you can take an HSA with you anywhere.

Ellevest's Sofia Figueroa recommends spending all your FSA money (which is often given out up front) while you have it. "Go to FSAstore.com and use that money, because you're going to lose it. Even everyday essentials like menstrual products and skin-care products, you can buy using your FSA dollars."

As for an HSA, it doesn't matter whether you're employed or not. "Your HSA is yours," says Donovan. "That's your money and travels with you. Even if you don't have insurance, you could use that HSA to pay for a co-pay at the doctor."

Who Can You Ask for Help?

Sarah Michalczuk, founder and CEO of Predictabill, also suggests calling your former company's HR department or benefits manager. Even if it's been a while since you left, "I think most benefit managers actually do want to help."

Insurance websites have navigators that can help people understand their insurance options, enroll in health plans, and help you find a doctor. Laura did this recently and was surprised by how fast and comprehensive the results were.

Also, if you suffer from a chronic or debilitating condition, contact the Patient Advocate Foundation (patientadvocate.org). "They can help you evaluate a plan. They're not going to choose it for you, but they can help you figure out what your options are," says Donovan.

Get In, Loser, We're Going Shopping

OK, this is the brain-melting part—there are a million health-care plans and precisely no universal help navigating them all. "There are no classes on shopping for health insurance," says Andy Hamilton, CEO of When, a health-care severance solution provider. "It's not something we do because we traditionally get it from our employer. So, when you lose your job, if you're like many people, this is the first time you've ever had to shop for health insurance on your own and it's at the most stressful, painful part of your career. You're worried about getting a new job. You're worried about putting food on the table. And, by the way, you have to sort through three hundred plans and find the ideal health insurance for you or pay a crazy premium."

The above paragraph alone probably sent you to urgent care. But keep breathing, we got you.

Your Options

- Join your partner's health insurance if they have it and you are eligible through marriage, domestic partnership, etc. (You can do this outside of the normal open enrollment window—November through mid-January—because being laid off is what is referred to as a Qualifying Life Event.) Have your partner talk to their benefits manager to see how much their premiums will increase if you join their plan.

- Join your parents' health insurance if you are under age twenty-six. Their premiums will also likely increase, but again, check how much.

- Sign up for Medicare if you are over sixty-four and a half years old.

- Sign up for Medicaid. You can see if you qualify at healthcare.gov.

- Go online to your state's open health-care marketplace and sign up for a plan.

- Sign up for a short-term plan.

- Sign up for COBRA.

Which Option Is Best for You?

First things first: "As a rule of thumb, you don't want to be paying more than 8 percent of your pre-tax income for health insurance," says Michalczuk. So, pull out that calculator.

List Your Doctors

Make a list of all of your doctors and check what insurance each one takes. They might all be different, so you will need to prioritize who you will use most. Does your trusted GP of ten years take Aetna but not Anthem? That's a key consideration.

Now, finding out about coverage isn't as easy as calling the receptionist at the doctor's office—they don't necessarily have all that detailed information just stored in their head. What they should have, though, is a list of insurance they accept that they can email you directly. (Laura got a wrong verbal answer on coverage from an office once and ended up with an out-of-pocket bill.)

So, check with *both* your doctor (provider) and insurance that the doctor is in network because either one of those could give you the wrong information. Donovan has a key tip: "If a provider is listed as in-network on your insurer's website, always take a screenshot because if they provide you with the wrong information, you can't be held liable for those out-of-network charges."

Go to Healthcare.gov or Research Private Platforms

Healthcare.gov will ask you to input your zip code and your income. Then it will send you down one of two paths: One, you pay full price or are eligible for subsidized plans. Two, you might qualify for Medicaid, which is free.

You can also use private and more user-friendly platforms like Predictabill, which will show what plans are available to you, how much they cost, and if the doctors you see regularly are covered by those plans.

Medicaid

Medicaid is a federal program that provides health insurance to eligible low-income individuals or those with specific healthcare needs. If you qualify for Medicaid, you need to back up your claim with documents: a letter confirming that you were laid off and your income is suspended. "You have to prove that you're not lying about your income because a human is going to look at it in those cases," says Michalczuk. The good thing? If you qualify for Medicaid, it covers you for a year.

Michalczuk gives an example of how to use this safety net: "You get laid off, maybe you have three weeks of severance. After your severance runs out, you go to healthcare.gov. It calculates that you have a 'go-forward' income of zero or less than five thousand dollars a year or something [depending on your state's requirements]. Bam, you're on Medicaid. That's free. Here's your Medicaid card in the mail, relax while you're looking for a job." Well, relax-ish!

If you want to renew your Medicaid after a year, you will need to report your income again. If you, God willing, now make too much money for Medicaid, you may still be eligible for subsidies.

Michalczuk says, "You should probably get on a silver plan. Those have lower deductibles [and cover approximately 70 percent of expenses]."

The irony of the whole confusing thing is, "The system is actually designed to work really well with life transitions," she adds. "It's just that there's no one there to tell you how that works."

Open Marketplace

Here's how to shop for one of the most complicated purchases of your life. Because you've lost your job, you can apply at any time, but remember again, if you want to make a change, open enrollment runs only from November 1 until January 15. Once you've made your choice, you can't change horses until then (Laura was stuck with shitty insurance for a year, but jumped to make a change as soon as the calendar hit November). That is, unless you have a Qualifying Life Event—birth, death of a dependent, divorce, marriage—or get a new job, where you can join your new company's health-care plan.

Marketplace Plans on Healthcare.gov

Marketplace plans cover "essential health-care benefits," like maternity care, mental health, prescription coverage, and emergency coverage. Marketplace plans differ from state to state.

First, type in your zip code and income level and you will be directed to various plans, listing their costs, offerings, and in-network doctors/providers. Every state has different local providers as well as big corporate ones. Depending on where you live and your budget, you could also qualify for tax benefits or subsidies.

Even though this process will congeal your brain, take some time with it. Don't just look at the big names like United or Blue Cross, says Michalczuk, as they might have designed a less substantial network for the marketplace because it's cheaper. "They want to sell plans, but it doesn't cover as much," she says.

"Do not discount the names you have not heard of," Michalczuk adds. "In New York City, for example, Health First and Fidelis have been around for decades and they're regional experts. They're really quite good." Also, look at the costs. You might be paying more for a name than what a plan actually gives you.

If you can't afford a $600-a-month marketplace plan right now, Donovan says: "When you are applying for that marketplace plan, you're putting in your own income. If you put it at zero, you're going to be able to find a zero-premium plan."

But let's say you find a new job and drop that plan in a few months. "You may owe more taxes at the end of the year because you ended up with a higher salary." But hell, that's a price worth paying if you end up in the hospital and your new employer pays the bill.

What Is COBRA Again?

It's not a snake, but it is slippery—and expensive. COBRA, the federal act passed in 1985, gives workers and their families the right to choose to continue health benefits for a limited time period. Basically, it's health insurance . . . insurance. You get to keep your employer coverage, but you pay a much higher premium (depending on your exit agreement with your employer). COBRA lasts for eighteen to thirty-six months, depending on different Qualifying Life Events (check with your state, your employer's benefits manager, and your provider to determine what those are).

Your premiums are going to jump by *a lot*. Usually, when you get fired, you will receive a letter in the mail explaining how much your COBRA premiums will be. Then you will have to figure out: one, if you can afford it, and two, if it's worth it.

Reasons to Stay on COBRA

COBRA allows you to keep your current health insurance plan, so all your doctors can stay the same, and any deductibles or out-of-pocket maximums will carry over. "The only reason I would recommend you stay on COBRA is if it's far along in your plan year and you've already met the deductible," says Donovan. "If you have more high costs coming, it might make sense to stay on that coverage (even though the premium will be expensive) because your out-of-pocket costs elsewhere would include starting over [with a new deductible]."

If you love your doctors, have a preexisting condition, or have a surgery coming up, COBRA provides continuity. Figueroa says, "If you are scheduled for a surgery and you've already mapped out all the costs or have particular health concerns and a team of medical professionals that really work well with you, sometimes it's worth paying more for COBRA coverage so you can maintain those systems."

Key Things to Know About COBRA

- Remember what Laura said about waiting for the card in the mail? If you choose to enroll in COBRA, you have to physically do it—i.e., sign the paperwork, set up a payment plan, etc. You are NOT automatically enrolled.

- It can be retroactively added for up to a certain amount of time, most commonly sixty days. Two months in fired-time goes by fast. Don't wait to enroll.

- You can quit COBRA at any time. "The second you stop paying your premiums and you lose coverage, that triggers a life event, enabling you to sign up for different insurance," explains Michalczuk. "You don't have to wait for open enrollment."

Some Health-Care Hacks

All from Caitlin Donovan, who just lowered our heart rate:

Prescriptions

- GoodRx, where you can see which pharmacy might be the least expensive for you.

- Copays.org, where you qualify based on your condition and income level.

- Cost Plus Drugs, where you can get a lot of generic medication at cost.

- Many drug companies, such as Pfizer, Merck, and Novartis, offer co-pay assistance. Check your medications and enroll in the drug company's co-pay assistance program, or call their helpline. If you are approved, you will receive a co-pay card or voucher. And it doesn't matter whether you have commercial insurance or not—you may find yourself a better deal.

Negotiate with Your Doctors

"It is 100 percent reasonable for you to go to your doctor and say, 'I just got laid off. This insurance will be expiring while I'm looking for my new options. Do you have a pay-in-cash option?' See if you can negotiate down to a better deal for yourself. Offices will be very receptive if you're telling them you can pay in cash. Or you can always ask for a payment plan."

If You're Thinking, "Screw It, I Don't Need No Health Care..."

Then, we repeat, you *have to* consider the worst-case scenario. "If someone says, 'I can't afford a marketplace plan' after a layoff, I'd say, 'How could you afford an emergency room visit?'" Which is kind of the worst touché ever.

And if the Worst Thing Happens (You End Up in the Hospital with a Giant Bill)

Do not pay your bill right away. "About half of the bills we see at the Patient Advocate Foundation have an error in them," says

Donovan. "The easiest way to check it is to wait. Always wait for your explanation of benefits [EOB] that comes in the mail. The EOB is that piece of paper that says 'This Is Not a Bill' on it. Most people just disregard it, but you shouldn't. Compare that to the bill, because if there's a discrepancy between those numbers, there's a mistake."

Challenge the Bill

Call your insurance company and your provider. They may try to bat the issue to the other, so the best thing you can do is get them on a three-way call, says Donovan. Ask direct questions: "I don't think I should be getting a bill for this. I think I'm being charged too much. Can you tell me what is going on?"

Ask for Financial Assistance

Many hospitals have financial assistance programs. Who knew? Because they'll never tell you. "You can always ask the billing department what you have to do to qualify for financial assistance." OK, you can go back to bed now.

Jennifer O'Connell & Rebecca Quinn

Jennifer O'Connell and Rebecca Quinn are co-founders of Velvet Hammer Media. They were both laid off from HBO Max when it merged with Discovery in 2022.

> "We've made a lot of men rich … It's our turn."

What Happened

JENNIFER O'CONNELL: Rebecca and I knew each other from our previous time together at Lionsgate. I was overseeing the unscripted side of the studio, and Rebecca had a production deal there. When I went to HBO Max in 2019, it was about a year before Max's launch. I had zero team, zero projects. We needed to start from scratch. That's when Rebecca called me.

REBECCA QUINN: Jen has always been a champion of women and people of color long before companies became invested in DEI [diversity, equity, and inclusion]. She was a mentor to me. I had no experience working at a network; I'd only been a producer. But I called her. I did that thing women do, "I'm sure you don't want to hire me. I'm sure you have other people that are better. But I just had to say that I would like to work with you at Max." And she goes, "You're hired."

O'CONNELL: We started working together, built the team, acquired shows, started development. We were busy, busy, busy, and then Covid hit, and our division was the one that could make things happen fast. So, we had a lot of weight on our shoulders to deliver, but it was so much fun because they trusted us, and we had the best time together coming up with ideas, making shows.

Together, we learned so much. I trust Rebecca with my life. It was just such a great relationship. We don't always agree, but that was part of the beauty of it. So, honestly, the hardest part about the job ending for us was not the actual job itself. It was recognizing that it would never be like that again.

When the merger between HBO Max and Discovery hit in 2022, there were signs that something was going down—meetings we weren't invited to, rumors around the industry. Our department overlapped with the new company—and all the new company did was unscripted and reality. So, logically, it made sense that there would be streamlining. We were like, OK, we can see this iceberg that we're headed toward. Everyone was very polite—business as usual, head down—but too many little red flags kept popping up.

You know the saying "Don't ask questions that you don't want the answer to"? Well, in this case, asking the questions and knowing the answers was exactly what we wanted. Whatever the outcome.

So, I walked into a meeting with someone who had the answers, and before I could even open my mouth, they said, "I can't lie to you; we thought maybe it could work out, but there isn't going to be a place for you." I said, "OK, what about the team?" The answer was, "No, everyone. We're shutting the whole thing down."

I walked out with a smile on my face, because my whole team was sitting there. And then I ran into Rebecca.

QUINN: I give Jen a knowing look. We tell everyone we're going to lunch. When we get into the elevator, I go, "Is it bad?" Jen says, "Yeah." I go, "Are we fired?" She goes, "Yeah." I say, "Is the whole team fired?" She goes, "Yeah." I go, "Let's go get a drink."

We went to a W hotel and got shots of [Don Julio] 1942 on the company card. I said to Jen, "This is really tough, but we're going to be OK, and we're going to start our own business." We had never talked about it before. I can't remember if it was before the shots or after.

I knew the firing was coming. It really was not a shock to me. It was a shock that Jen had the balls to go into the top person's office and basically be like, "What's the deal?"

But I had been thinking, and I don't say this to brag, we were successful. Compared to some of the other top streamers, we had done a lot and done really well, and the town sort of knew that.

So, when we got fired, it was this weird thing where it was the opposite of schadenfreude. People felt for us. They were like, "Oh shit. These women work really hard and then, damn!" Just like that. It's sort of like the Ghost of Christmas Future.

I, of course, didn't know that at the time when I said we should start a company; all I knew is that Jen's the best person I'd ever worked with in the business, the most respected. I just wanted to keep doing what we were doing—to be in her orbit and not go away. I thought that we could do that.

O'CONNELL: We're very confident. Which is a blessing; it's blind confidence sometimes, but it's just because we've been doing this for so long. We've seen the cycles and what happens to other people. There was a long waiting period before we could do what we wanted to do. The waiting to get started was the hardest.

What Next

QUINN: We got ourselves prepared. I began taking online business classes because I'd never started a business before. And by online business classes, I mean that I was watching YouTube videos posted by Harvard and Stanford business schools. I wasn't, like, officially *in* them, but I did study them for six months. I'm like, "I got an MBA, Jen!"

A lot of men were telling us that it was the absolute wrong time to start an unscripted television business, it was starting to take a turn, the purses were tightening, they weren't buying as many shows. Objectively, it probably was the worst time to start a business. But we believed we had something to offer that was different. There are very few production companies led by women, and even fewer led by a woman and a woman of color. What they didn't understand is that we had a different POV that we thought the timing was perfect for.

O'CONNELL: We put together a business plan. We were meeting a lot of people who gave advice—some great, some not so great.

QUINN: I would say 90 percent of people told us not to do it, "But if you want to do it, we'll invest."

Velvet Hammer Media was announced in The Hollywood Reporter *in summer 2022 with this quote: "At this pivotal moment in our business, we're excited to bet on ourselves and leverage our complementary strengths."*

QUINN: We were told not to do certain things. A publicist told us to be more generic [less focused on who we are personally], but we said, that's just not who we are. We are betting on ourselves, and we're going to come out of the gate aggressive.

O'CONNELL: We've worked for so many different companies in our careers, and frankly, we've made a lot of men rich. In my mind—and I know Rebecca feels the same way—it's our turn. If we're going to spend the time grinding away, it has to be for ourselves. It was time. I was just turning fifty and it was a bit like, God, am I starting a company now?!

QUINN: We were deciding whether to use our own money to fund the company or bring on investors. We met with nine different investors. We got offered a deal from eight of them. So, every meeting, we got more and more confident. By the end we were like, "Here are the terms we will accept; here's what we want to get paid. You're going to have a minority stake." We just learned all of these things as we went.

And when one guy who was mansplaining said, "What do you know about this?" I said, "Well, I went to business school."

O'CONNELL: Over the years, I've thought about starting a company. I always wanted a partner, never had the right person, until Rebecca came along. Being able to go into meetings together, knowing that if you're having an off day, she's going to help, and vice versa. We bring different things to the table. You know, one day I'm velvet and she's the hammer. Another day, I'm the hammer.

QUINN: I've had no problem pitching friends at networks and streamers for business. We're like, "Guys, we won't let you down. Give us a series, and we'll come and pitch you twenty shows. You're going to pick one; you're going to love one." It's just a totally different swagger.

We got fired; we're playing loose. Everyone is telling us it's not the time to pitch, no one has the money, the writers' strikes, all the excuses. We have no excuses. We don't give up. We just grind every day. We can outwork anyone; we really can. It may not be healthy, but we love it.

What We Learned

QUINN: Losing that job at Max was the best thing that happened to me career-wise.

O'CONNELL: Same! I'm so much happier. And healthier, too. I've learned you can't control everything, and as a control freak, that's really hard for me. This merger, as I said before, was like an iceberg we were headed straight toward, and there was literally nothing I could do about it. It was out of my control, and it's not personal. It was a business decision. Just being able to acknowledge that and not take it to heart helps.

The other thing is having a partner like Rebecca. We keep each other optimistic, and if one of us is having a bad day, the other picks her up. When we're "in the room," it is nothing but energy and excitement and optimism. We get passes on the shows we pitch every day. We couldn't care less. We just like moving forward and not letting any negativity stick to us. We don't need that heaviness weighing us down.

QUINN: The biggest thing I've learned is how much confidence can change your life. We've worked in this business for twenty-five years. It's shocking that this is the first time I've ever felt professionally confident. That you can walk away from being fired and be better for it. That gave me the confidence to know that if our production company doesn't work for whatever reason, we'll figure something out. Together we can do anything; that's my new attitude. It's not just one shot. We got a lot of shots.

O'CONNELL: To be in control of our own destiny is amazing and liberating and wonderful.

QUINN: I really believe that getting fired is not a bad thing. While it's hard and emotional, you need to flip the script and think about it as an opportunity.

O'CONNELL: I had a lot of women call me after they had been fired, because the industry is contracting. And I was like, "Welcome to the club! The water's warm here." Call someone who's been fired. Call another woman who's been through it the day it happens, because they will make you feel better. Don't be shy. Don't sit alone in a dark room and bury yourself under the covers. Talk to people and own it. Say, "I just got fired. What should I do?"

QUINN: When women can't own their firing, it's because they're holding on to this shame that they did something wrong. They didn't do anything wrong. And I think women struggle to separate what's out of their control with what's in their control. It's such a painful, complicated situation when that happens to you.

Feeling shame is a waste of time. And it certainly doesn't help anything. Instead, it's so liberating to get fired and think, "What a loss for you guys."

Sallie Krawcheck

Sallie Krawcheck is the co-founder of women's investment platform Ellevest. She was fired as CFO of Citigroup in 2008 and in 2011, as head of Merrill Lynch's global wealth management division.

"We're more resilient than we give ourselves credit for."

What Happened

The two days I got kicked out of my jobs would end up being the best days of my life. If you don't want me, I don't want to be there. I have a great family, and there are other business opportunities that I'd like to go after. Thank you for letting me know you don't want me, so I can go after those better opportunities.

I got booted twice. Not only am I an OG, but I'm an OG all-star. The first one, at Citi in 2008, was a long time coming. You could just watch it steamrolling down the street. So, I wasn't that surprised with that one. At Bank of America, where I was hired in 2009, my charge had been to turn around Merrill Lynch after Bank of America bought it during the subprime crisis. And we did! I put in a new team, and the business in almost every metric was healthy and performing and improving, gaining share, and beating the plan. So, in 2011, when I was called in and told, thanks for the reorg, we're going to give it to another person now that you've turned it around for us, I was shocked.

I've worked in places where I was wired in. But I wasn't in the in crowd at Bank of America. I didn't know what was going to happen in meetings before it happened. The CEO never stopped by my office, sat in a chair, put his feet up on my desk, and said, "Can we brainstorm this?" But the overachieving little girl in me was like, "But I was getting A's! I did what I was supposed to do!" I was stunned. When he said, "You'll be let go," I think I literally said, "*Who, me?!*"

When I left Citi, the only surprise was how I found out about it. I was alone in my office, and those Wall Street offices always had CNBC playing in the background. I was doing something at my desk, and I turned and saw a woman on the screen who I did not immediately recognize wearing what I thought was a pretty terrific-looking suit. It said she was leaving her company. And I looked at it, and I thought, "Great suit, tough day . . . *OH MY GOD, IT'S ME!*" Then the phone lit up, and the texts lit up, and the emails lit up. And they hadn't told me yet.

A similar thing happened at Bank of America, where they let me know and then told the media within fifteen minutes. It was terrible. My dad was at the gym and saw it on the TV before I could call him. Maybe it's typical Wall Street protocol, but there is a certain level of cruelty to it. They were protecting themselves—if they can put the story out first, and I don't get in front a bit, and if I don't call... I know the score. But it still stung.

At Bank of America, after the CEO told me about the "restructuring," I thought, "Do I shake his hand?" He did not move to shake, so I just sort of wandered out of his office. That one stays with me—that he didn't shake my hand. That was weird. The other thing is they had scheduled a dinner for my direct reports that night. The whole thing was orchestrated. So, I walked out with my bag... and there's everybody going to dinner.

I called my husband and said, "Keep the kids away from the TV. Here we go, again..." Years later, I found out he told them, "Be nice to your mom tonight." When I got home, I went right to the library, sat down, and started drinking. What is there to do? Cry?

You certainly realize it's not a family. It's a business. The first firing hurt the most because I really loved the job, the people, the team. I just felt like I poured everything into it, and so that one felt more emotional. As I said, I was never part of the in crowd at Bank of America, so it was less emotional in that way.

What Next

After I was knocked out of Citi, a journalist told me that men could come back from a big Wall Street firing, but women could not. I also remember the head of a search firm telling me that I would be on slates for jobs—but I would never get them. I was on the slates because of diversity, because I was a woman. But I would never get the jobs because the very fact that I had been kicked out meant that I was a troublemaker of some kind. So, I had all this negative stuff coming at me. Part of me was like, "He's just wrong."

I had a memorable moment with a work friend, sometime after leaving Citi, whom I hadn't seen in months. He said, "Oh my gosh! I just had a project, a company we were going to buy; you would have been perfect to run its wealth management business. I don't know why I didn't think of you!" And I thought I was pretty obvious, but then I realized: out of sight, out of mind.

Too many people told me, "You have to do something fast because the opportunities come right at the beginning." Then they degrade pretty quickly. That's terrifying advice. How do you engage? When do you engage? How do you stay top of mind for people so that when something comes along, they do think of you?

Another big one for me was, how do I introduce myself at a cocktail party? What do I say I do? "I used to run . . ." "I'm between successes . . ." If you do the job, and they go in a different direction, if it's a new boss—all bets are off. But breaking the ice and owning it—and owning it right up front—means you don't carry the same burden. So, when I got fired, I decided to just be honest and forthright about it, and find the good things in it.

That said, I remember going out to lunch with a woman after she had been fired. I came with different ideas for her. There was a board looking for someone, a startup looking for someone, so I had suggestions for her, and I was happy to make the connections. But she spent the entire lunch telling me how she had *not* been fired: her boss said this and then she said this and the boss said this. I left with such a broken heart. I didn't think any less, more, or differently of her because of this thing that happened. I didn't care. But I was never able to give her the recommendations.

It was a few years from the "Don't let the door hit you on the way out" moment to when we launched Ellevest in 2014 [Krawcheck's investment platform focuses on the unique financial circumstances of women—from career breaks when having children and income gaps with men to planning for retirement], but I was busy the whole time. I was fortunate enough to be able to give myself time, and smart enough to take the time.

I would ask people: "What would you do if you were me?" I got back this broad range of answers. "You should go to a hedge fund." That totally left me cold. "You should start an asset management company that leverages your relationships with your financial advisers." Ah, OK, let me think about that one. I looked into going into government. I would sort of gauge, does that make me feel excited? And I tried to be really introspective about what mattered. Is it money that matters? Is it a mission that matters? Is it intellectual curiosity? Is it being global? Which of those is important to me? We have to give our subconscious the opportunity to speak.

I would also write a lot during these times. Things like: What do I want to be known for? What makes me happy? I would write in the morning, when I was waking up, and at night, over a glass of wine, to try to get rid of the chatter and get to the core.

If I'm going to be honest, what took me so long to land on a [female finance] direction was partly due to internalized sexism. People would say, you should start an investing firm for women.

But my immediate reaction was, for women?! That's very junior varsity and I'm in the big leagues—I'm with the guys. There had been initiatives for women, but they were all lightweight. They were marketed to women as opposed to serving women. I had these patriarchal layers that I had to go through to get to Ellevest. I could have saved myself eighteen months.

I always come back to Girls Who Code CEO Reshma Saujani's quote: "Boys are taught to be brave and girls are taught to be perfect." I just think that captures so much. As a woman, when you get fired, that's not perfection. So, the shame of the whole thing is a lot.

Along the way, there were these moments. I would carry an Ellevest bag to the airport and women would stop me. "Are you an Ellevest client? I'm an Ellevest client." There was one woman in Austin, Texas, who cried and said, "You changed my life." There was one woman in an elevator in the Flatiron District who said, "I just closed my account. I took my money out—I'm going to graduate school with it."

Things like that never happened at the big firms. The other great moment was when we hit $2 billion of assets under management and rang the bell of the New York Stock Exchange in March 2024. To go to that bastion of maleness and see it plastered with Ellevest signage—that was fun.

What I Learned

My best career advice is to invest. A big difference between men and women is the gender pay gap, but it really is the gender wealth gap driven by the gender investing gap. That's a lot of gaps! Women tend to save their money and men tend to invest their money. But look at the stock market: historically, it has increased an average of 10 percent a year. That difference, when you combine it with compounding, where you start to earn money on your money and money on your money, that's all she wrote. Not investing as much as men do has cost women hundreds of thousands—for some, millions—of dollars over the course of their lives. So, that is a big difference on the day you get fired.

When you're in a job, I would start with a 401(k) and see what you need to invest to get the employer match [it varies significantly between companies and also by the seniority of your role]. I would be trying to invest some amount out of every paycheck. If you can only afford to contribute 1 percent, do 1 percent. If you can do up to 10 percent, do up to 10 percent, and get those recurring deposits into an investment fund so that money works for you. And if you do that, on the day you get fired, you'll end up a lot more confident. And if you haven't, you'll want to take a step back. Do you have an emergency fund? Do you have three to six months of take-home pay? Hopefully you've already built it, but if you haven't, get started. If you've got money in the stock market, you might take it out to put it in a bank because you're going to need it in the short term.

You may want to negotiate your package. We, as women, we're still taught *this is it*. But is there more money on the table? Is there more health care that you can get? Really think about negotiating every step of the way.

We're more resilient than we give ourselves credit for. Fortunately, I knew there was going to be dinner on the table. I knew the kids were going to go to school the next day; I knew we weren't going to lose the house. I was in a privileged set of circumstances.

There are a hundred opportunities to be successful every day: you're just not looking for them. If you can get yourself straight on what you want to do—that's the tough part—then start doing it and grab those opportunities. I would have said to my fired self: it's going to be OK; it's going to be a lot of work. But there are many different ways to be successful.

At the end of the day, nobody else cares. Nobody's talking about you. Did they talk about you when they heard it? Sure. Were they on to the next thing immediately? Absolutely. People care about themselves. They don't remember. Just let it go.

9

Mental Health

How to Grieve; How to Get on With It

For many people, their identity is wrapped up in their job, so when that job is lost, their identity is threatened, too. In Australia, it's called "chucking a wobbly." In the United States, try "freaking out" or "losing your shit."

(In all seriousness, if the loss of your job has led you to experience an extreme mental health crisis, please know you're not alone. Losing a job can take people to dark places, but help, and community, is out there. Reach out to friends, family, or to a lifeline like 988 in the US or equivalent for support.)

The key message of this chapter is: *do not attach your personal value to your work!* But we're not robots; we know that's far easier said than done. That feeling of being displaced, of being professionally and financially vulnerable, is frightening. After all, you had a place to go every day (physically or remotely), relationships you made, pals you gossiped with at lunch, habits you formed.

Losing your job is like a breakup, and just like a breakup, a jarring change in your daily rituals can throw you for a loop. Who are you without it? Laura and Kristina's industry, fashion, does a better job than most of placing value on the most superficial things: where you're invited, what you wear, and literally—when it comes to a fashion show—where you sit.

For both of us, we found that deliberately and publicly staying in our hard-earned worlds was helpful, even if it made us feel queasy in our tummies (sometimes queasier than others; it's OK to feel yucky and go home early—we've both done it). Laura was laid off in the middle of New York Fashion Week, so she strategically went to the Proenza Schouler fashion show the very next day. While, yes, she'd been fired, she was still *invited*, and after all her years in magazine publishing, she'd earned the right to be there. The entire New York fashion industry was in that room, so she put on a chic suit, squared her shoulders, and walked right to her front-row seat—receiving a few hugs and I-can't-believe-its on the way.

After her canning, Kristina put on her best black pantsuit, went to a big, fancy Tiffany & Co. store opening party in Midtown, and straight up told people she'd been fired. Champagne glasses jiggled with the shock. Some people thought she had left on her own accord. Not so. (It was a good reminder that people are too caught up in their own dramas to dwell on yours.) So, she fired herself up (pun so intended) and worked the room, connecting with key industry players and thanking them for their support.

"This doesn't define me. This doesn't define me," played over and over in her head.

Of course, these are niche media-industry examples, and nothing needs to be this swish; it could be setting up coffee dates at your local Starbucks. (Absolutely give yourself a brief wallow break, but you need to strike while the pink slip is still hot and your firing is top of other people's minds.) Stay in the world. Be visible. Or just visible enough. Laura calls it "Proof of Life." Proof you're open to what comes next.

And honestly, seeing other people, just being in the world, will make you feel better. (Absolutely *nobody* feels jazzier after spending days alone in their apartment.)

Of course, when you're "out there," there will be *a lot* of conversations. People might tell you to have a plan, but more important than that is having a sense of humor. (This is also your sense of preservation.) The two of us—socially and broadly—went about telling all sorts of people we'd been fired, often to audible gasps at the idea that we would be so frank about the situation (again, there's that odd retro streak in women's behavior about this sort of stuff). But each time we told the story honestly, the stronger we felt, ironically. Our two ducks in the pond were still paddling, goddamn it.

If you find that your identity and your job were too enmeshed, getting fired is a wake-up call to set some boundaries between the two at your next job. Two things we found helpful: One, have an identity outside of your job (be it on social media, a sports team, or at the local pottery workshop). Two, friends! Real ones, not fair-weather ones who hung with you during the good times and then receded into the fog. If you've worked hard and been nice, we promise you, hand on heart, these folks are the—extremely uncool—minority. If you lose some . . . losers, it's just life's editing process. Keep what you want, delete what you don't. And most importantly, take whatever steps you need to shore up your mental health.

Take a Deep Breath

Remember in the old movies, when our anxious (but gorgeous) heroine breathed into a paper bag? Kinda like that. Bucky Keady, HR expert, advises, "Give yourself some time. If it's a week or two weeks, and you want to cry, have at it. It's sort of like that scene with Diane Keaton in *Something's Gotta Give*." (Kids, look it up: Keaton writes an entire Broadway play while heaving with sobs for weeks. You don't have to write a play, by the way—just sobbing is fine.)

Give yourself some time, because knee-jerk decisions, especially ones made while freaking out, are generally not the best ones. "Try to calm yourself down because diving into the next step when you're buzzing with anxiety may lead to choices that you make in haste," says Ron Lieber, the *New York Times* money columnist. "The best thing that you can do for yourself is take a week off—or even just a day—and think about what work made you most happy and least happy over the course of your career. What could you do next time to increase the happiness and decrease the unhappiness?" See? It's like math for your dreams.

Jill Mizrachy, group people lead at management consultancy

Booz Allen Hamilton, argues that having some time, just in itself, is a luxury. "See this as the opportunity that it is. All of us become quite insular in our work because we are focused. We have deliverables, workflows, timelines, deadlines. We are trying to manage life and everything else. All of a sudden, in some ways, you're free."

Did you hear that? Free! Give that gift to yourself.

It's OK to Grieve

You just lost something that you spent eight (at least!) hours a day doing, five days a week. The majority of your waking hours. Not to mention all the time projects, deadlines, and office politics (such a waste of brainpower, by the way) spent rattling around your head. You're not just losing a job; you're breaking a habit: a routine you've become accustomed to every day. For the two of us, it was being yanked out of a super-ritualistic industry (we spent two full months of the year going to fashion shows—yes, we know that is deranged) that made for the biggest shock. For a little while it felt a bit like, "They're all having fun without me."

Career coach Phoebe Gavin says, "It's important to label a layoff as a traumatic event. It is a betrayal of a contract. You sign an employment agreement for a full-time permanent position, and yes, they have that little paragraph about being an at-will employee, but the assumption is that it is a *permanent* position. That's literally what it's called.

"So, when you're laid off, especially if it's the first time it's happened to you, it feels like an extreme betrayal, especially because you look back on the time that you spent at that employer, whether it was months or years, and all you can think about is all the sacrifices and all the time and all the trade-offs and all the frustration, all the sleepless nights, all the late hours and weekends that you put into that company to fulfill your end of the bargain. That betrayal is deeply harmful, and I strongly encourage anyone who's experienced a layoff to be really thoughtful about how you can care for your mental health and your emotional health and heal from that as you move into your next scenario."

If getting fired hits you so hard that you have trouble getting out of bed, have a think about how much of yourself you invested in the job: Was it a little *too* much? Maybe that was less than healthy, in retrospect? "If it's your person that just got attacked so deep, it can reflect that there are other elements of life that aren't as strong as they could be," says Keady. "If somebody's living a rich life, or has a great partner, for the most part, they're not as shattered." Which takes us to our next point...

You Are Not Your Job

Écoutez et répétez! Listen and repeat! (Don't worry, it doesn't have to be in French.) We've said earlier and we'll say it again: do not attach your value to your work. If you merge yourself too closely with your job and derive all of your identity and status from it, if you lose it, you will, well... lose it.

Today, at industry events and the odd fashion show she still attends, Laura walks around doing unsolicited "you got this" TED Talks all the time. Recently, an editor friend complained to her about keeping mentally afloat in the declining magazine business:

"This is so *hard*." Laura launched into her speech about all of her friend's incredible abilities that she could rely on without letting this job suck the life out of her. "You don't need it," Laura said.

Her friend replied, "*Don't I?*"

That's the most challenging, most poignant part. To save yourself, you have to reset your brain a little, to know that your *individual* skills, experience, and personality are all the things that make you distinctive in the workplace. And when you leave (even if that wasn't the plan) you take all of that with you. *That* is *you*, not your job. It takes work to train yourself to think this way, but it makes you so much less vulnerable to the ill winds of industries you can rarely control.

That said, of course, layoffs *feel* personal. There is someone sitting with you, or Zooming with you, telling you that you are no longer employed. While often others in your group or at your level still are. "We tend to assign human values to companies because when we are in a company, we are working with people. But those relationships are facilitated and managed by our economic relationship to our employer. They don't work the same way as regular human relationships," says Gavin.

If you are enmeshed too closely with your workplace on social media, that's a warning sign, too. "I'm always concerned when I'm on LinkedIn or social media and someone's personal brand on social media is completely about their company. Because the moment that the company decides to separate from you, if it's for a good reason, bad reason, or financial decisions, then you feel like you've lost a huge part of your identity," says workplace mental health strategist Natasha Bowman (who also wrote *Crazy AF: How to Go from Being Burned Out, Unhappy & Unmotivated to Reclaiming Your Mental Health at Work*).

"What we need to stop doing is completely merging our personal identities with our workplace identities," Bowman adds. "Separating that identity is one of the best ways to protect your mental health. We are still very valuable. And the only thing we were doing was lending our credibility, our value, and our talents to the organization. That keyword there is *lend*. Not give."

"If you *are* your job and you get fired, then who are you?" asks Katherine Morgan Schafler, psychotherapist and author of *The Perfectionist's Guide to Losing Control*. "Hanging your whole identity onto *anything* external is precarious, at best. Everything changes. If these external components become your personhood, you can feel worthless if they shift. It's exhausting to orient yourself to how you're performing at work; you can't be centered if what you're centering yourself on is outside of you."

If you have PTSD from getting fired—which, sadly, so many do—that's also understandable. It's yet another argument for giving yourself time. Bowman says, "A lot of us suffer from PTSD from toxic work environments." So, if you're starting a new job, those shitty feelings can stay with you. "That means you are analyzing every word, every behavior, every movement at this new job because you haven't fully digested and healed from your former employer. You've got to take time to recover. Otherwise, you're going to carry that weight with you and you're not going to show up as your best self."

And remember: you control your story, your timeline, and your future, not your former employer. "It's important to understand that getting fired is one data point in a long, long story. A story in which you control the narrative," Morgan Schafler adds. "You may not be able to control whether you get fired or not, but you can control how you construct meaning around the events in your life."

Essentially, what happened to you might feel huge right now, but be sure to put it into the context of your life as a whole—hey now, it just got smaller, didn't it? And apply some ego while you're at it: Why give your former employer, or your negative experience, any power over you at all? What did any of them do to earn that? Nothing. It's like that ball of shame—do *not* carry it.

What's Your Motivation?

You know, like the method actors say. (We are not suggesting this as a career path, but hey, if you're into that.) *What makes you happy; what makes you less so?* Think like a kid. Because kids don't have jobs messing with their pure little brains. Were there professions you were curious about but were too locked into yours to think about? Write them down! Reach out to people who can introduce you to contacts in different industries to learn more about them. Are you a risk-taker, or do you crave security? This thinking might not spark a full career change but steer you toward environments that are more supportive of your interests.

Executive recruiter Kristy Hurt says, "This is a moment in time. Think of it as an opportunity. Get excited about what could come next, because the opportunities are endless. It's really up to you what you want to do next, where you want to put your energy and effort. It should be something you feel really excited about." See, listen to that inner kid!

Now, these next suggestions are a little bit woo-woo, but they might help:

Make an Emotional Map

Morgan Schafler suggests, "Decide how you want to feel during different parts of the day—write or draw what that would look like, then move in the direction of your map. For example, if you want to feel energized in the morning, write something that energizes you. For some people that's working out; for other people it's energizing to connect with your bestie. For me, solitude gives me energy, so I'd draw a woman alone in a room, writing at my desk with a hot tea. Make a map for different parts of the day. When you feel lost, follow the map. If you're living your everyday life in a way that feels good and energizing, the bigger answers aren't far behind. Work on the little things, and the big things will catch up to you."

What's Your Intention?

"Get clarity on the intention behind the work you do and do your best to detach from the job titles themselves," says Morgan Schafler. "When you figure out what your intention is, embody that intention." Is it to make art? To help people? Or, is it to make a shit-ton of money? Figure out what genuinely drives you.

She didn't call it her "intention," but Laura realized early on that being around people, stimulated by their company and their ideas, made her feel both excited and super engaged. This led to a career in media, originally sparked as a fourteen-year-old waitress talking to her adult customers. She still gets a high after a great conversation and starts immediately thinking of ways to work with that person. (Her team at *InStyle* would laugh that she would book someone she met at dinner the night before for the magazine.) Same goes for now: all of Laura's most exciting collaborations tend to stem from people she meets socially, rather than some rigid Grand Plan.

Growing up, Kristina's reading ranged from the adventures at *Sweet Valley High* to the suburban intrigues of Ann M. Martin's *Baby-Sitters Club* and Judy Blume's teenage dramas—later adding a steady, more sophisticated (or so she liked to think) pulse of Danielle Steel's drama. She was also, of course, a baby subscriber to *Mademoiselle* and *Seventeen*, eventually graduating to the polished pages of *Vogue*.

In ninth grade, she found her way into an Introduction to Journalism class. A summer spot in Northwestern's Medill Cherubs program, college at NYU's Gallatin School, and a few starter gigs in media later, Kristina knew that she loved words but didn't need to be the one to write them. So, she became an editor—a curator of ideas. And this wasn't just a career path; it was a highway, one where she could follow her intuitional GPS. Her destination? The center of the cultural conversation. She's kept the pedal to the metal ever since.

There's a Whole World Out There—Explore It

People who work in media, retail, service—anyone who engages with a ton of different people daily—often say their career is their hobby, because there is so much diverse stimuli every day. But when that stimuli drops off, you may find yourself in trouble. Which is why it's so helpful to have passions outside of your work. Do you like to garden? Play tennis? Travel? Are you a sports or current affairs addict? Hell, do you have a lifetime devotion to *The Real Housewives* and BravoCon?

Also, take an inventory of your friends: Are you still in touch with pals from high school, college—any of your "eras"—or did you let them lapse? These are the folks who are going to shore you up and remind you that there was another whole *you* before this job, and there will be another one after. All of these things are your gateway to the broader world.

"Ensure you have passions outside of your work, which is really hard sometimes for women," Bowman says. "When we start to achieve professional success, we often leave behind other things we are passionate about, that give us purpose." It's not the work/life balance per se, but "harmonizing work and life so if one isn't serving its full purpose, we have the other to fall back on." If you have your scales reasonably aligned, "Your mind isn't fully filled with what we lost in terms of our job." Blessedly, you will have other things to think about.

Bowman remembers her own mental health crisis during the Covid pandemic. "I loved my career so much, no matter what job I was in or who I was working for. That was all that I enjoyed in life. I never paused to pursue other passions outside of work. So, when the quarantine happened, I was in HR and nobody was doing anything HR-related during that time. Even though I was working full-time, I was stagnant. I not only lost that sense of self-worth, I didn't have other interests to engage in."

Without sounding too twee about it, it can also be highly beneficial to your mental health to spend some time helping people less fortunate, as it gives you somewhere to go and some purpose and structure to your day, knowing you helped make a positive difference in someone else's. Bowman adds, "Volunteer at a nonprofit. Get up, take a shower, get dressed like you're going to work. Go do something to feel like you're contributing to society."

Do Not Shut the World Out!

As we said at the beginning of this chapter, what really helped us was being out in the world, not retreating from it. Seeing people, being social, and, above all, being frank about what happened to us helped swiftly chip away at doubt and insecurity. If you've planted the seeds (i.e., you've done work and been kind), people will show up for you. It's really kind of wild.

Bowman says, "A lot of times we feel alone because we don't like to tell people, 'Oh, I've been fired.'" (What this entire book is trying to remedy!) "We're embarrassed. But there are plenty of people who are going through the same thing as you are. Find a support network that can identify with you and help you through it, so you feel less alone. That sense of connection and belonging outside of the workplace is paramount to your healing in between."

Morgan Schafler concurs: "Connect to people who make you feel strong and safe, people who believe in you and see your current circumstance as an event, not a commentary on who you are. Connect to your body by nourishing yourself with nutritious foods, moving (walking counts), and trying your best to sleep well. Try a new route for your daily walk. Listen to new music. Connect to a new mentor. Start building newness in your life. I know it sounds cheesy, but . . . you're in a winter but start planting the seeds for spring. Don't expect your life to change right away, or even in a couple months, or even a year. Change takes time."

Keady adds, "Talk to your partner. Talk to your bestie. Find somebody who loves you. Talk to them." Hugging and kissing a cute little pet is also not to be underrated.

That said, if it's too much, it's more than OK to take a social break from your work pals. It's not super helpful to stay relentlessly clued in to what's happening back at the office. This is an unseemly metaphor, but it's like picking a scab: it will never heal. Your friends will understand if you need to take some time away and hard reset your head. You can giggle at what Douchey Dave said in the meeting . . . in six months. But by then, you won't even care. And which one was Dave?

Kristina is the first to admit this was harder for her than for Laura. She couldn't resist getting drawn into the gossip about her former colleagues. The intentions were good—friends would tattle to make her feel things weren't the same without her, that the office had lost its magic. But instead of comfort, they left her feeling worse. Each piece of gossip served as a sharp reminder that she was no longer part of that world and deepened her sense of disconnection. It was a lesson learned the hard way: sometimes the best way to heal is to unplug completely.

Cut Out Social Media if It's Feeling Toxic

Social media, as we all know (or *should* know by now), is life's highlight reel: the spiritual home of FOMO. When you're feeling low, everybody is having a better time than you! Everybody is better looking than you! Everyone has more money and more fun stuff than you! We know this feeling is irrational, and this relentless billboard is a pile of overfiltered BS, but it still worms its way into your head. Even if you're the most rational person in the world, it's insidious.

So, if social media is doing you more harm than good, remove those apps for a while. It's just *Groundhog Day* anyway—when you're ready to log back in, it will be more of the same.

"Maybe take a break from social media because a lot of times people are talking about all of their achievements and finding new jobs, and we start to think, 'Well, what's wrong with me? How come I'm not finding a new job?'" says Bowman. "Give yourself grace and time to find the right role. Don't compare your journey to someone else's."

And remember, they're exaggerating anyway. Facetuning not just their faces, but their lives.

But with all of that said . . .

Don't Numb Your Feelings

This is America! We love ourselves a shrink! Morgan Schafler says, "Something I always tell people is, 'If you're wondering if you should talk to a therapist, that's your cue to go to therapy.'

Also look out for numbing behaviors that are showing up in a patterned way. Numbing is any activity you engage in to avoid feeling what you're feeling. It doesn't make you feel good; it makes you feel nothing. Typical numbing behaviors are regularly binge-watching TV in a way that makes you feel gross, drinking to an extent you feel is too much, overeating, getting sucked up into relationship drama that distracts you, etc."

In short, it's OK to numb yourself for a little while—geez, lie on your face, if it helps. Get one of those big sleep creases that makes you look like a tough guy after a knife fight. Just don't remain numb for too long.

Tarana Burke

Tarana Burke is the founder and chief vision officer of me too. Movement. She was fired from her position of managing director at Art Sanctuary in 2013.

> "I kept thinking, 'You've been carrying other people's visions to fruition for too long.'"

What Happened

I've been working in nonprofits since I was thirteen. This is what I know, what I love. In 2008, I started working in Philadelphia at a nonprofit organization called Art Sanctuary, an important Black arts and cultural institution. Each year we would hold this big cultural festival in celebration of Black writing.

If we ended up in the red at the end of the year, the founder of the organization had access to some resources and would cut a check to help cover the loss. It wasn't a sustainable model. We knew she was stepping down soon, so she asked me if I wanted to take on the role of executive director [the highest job in the organization]. I didn't want it, though. Instead, I wanted to plug into doing my own work. [Burke had started #MeToo, dedicated to the healing of victims of sexual violence, in 2006, and was starting to think about devoting more time to it.]

The founder retired and the board hired a new executive director. I met Dani Ayers—now CEO of me too. Movement—at Art Sanctuary. We worked in tandem: I ran all the programs and managed the staff and she did all of the operations; we were as thick as thieves. And we both realized that fundraising for the organization was declining steadily.

Dani and I kept a really close eye on the budget. We kept saying to the new executive director, "If we don't watch this, we're going to be in real danger soon." So, she was like, "I know! We'll have a gala," as if that would solve the problem.

In the nonprofit world, galas are a death blow. Small organizations' galas end up raising little if any money, as they cost so much to throw. But she decided we were going to raise $2 million. Dani and I kept saying, "This is not going to work."

We spent $85,000 on this gala and got barely any sponsors. We ended up making $17,000.

By now it's 2013, and we are getting ready for our annual festival, the Celebration of Black Writing, held each year over Memorial Day weekend. In March, we had a board meeting. Dani and I had put together a presentation noting that Art Sanctuary would run out of money by June. It was dire. In response, we got a "Thank you very much. We appreciate you."

A month goes by, and we don't hear anything. The executive

director goes on a cruise. We're in the office, and I get a call from the head of our board, who says, "Hey, we'd like to meet with the staff. But with you first."

I thought they wanted to go over an agenda or something like that. But they're like, "We've gone over everything you and Dani gave us, thank you. This is going to be really difficult to manage going forward. So, we're relieving you of your duties."

I was like, "Excuse me?!" No warning, no nothing. They put it in the language of "laying off." They fired everybody one by one, apart from one person. It was effective immediately—we had to leave by the end of the day. I had worked there for five years.

I was so angry. You can't come into this office we've all worked at for years and tell us to leave at the end of the day. I gathered the team, and we wrote one ol' goodbye letter. We all sent it at the same time and cc'd our entire contact list.

What Next

That first week after being let go, I was livid. I just could not believe it. It was such a cowardly thing to do. I had poured so much into this job. And then when I reached out to the founder, she just was like, "You know, these things happen."

I was worried about money, health care, all of that. I didn't have a source of income. And if I'm completely honest, I was also cut off from my position. We did all these big, visible cultural events. There was concern about money, but I could always get a job. But it was also my status. That was just gone.

They ended up hiring a consultant to finish coordinating the event. But here's some beautiful karma. Ntozake Shange, who wrote *For Colored Girls Who Have Considered Suicide / When the Rainbow Is Enuf* was to be honored that night, along with Valerie Simpson from Ashford & Simpson.

Ntozake and I had a relationship from some prior work. So, when the consultant called people about the event, they were like, "Who are you? Where's Tarana?" Ntozake called me, and I said, "I don't work there anymore."

The day of the event, Ntozake came to my building. I said, "I'm not going," and she said, "Oh, the hell you ain't. You're coming as my guest. Or I'm not going up on that stage."

The look on the consultant's face when I got out of the limo with Ntozake was priceless. I was like, "I'm Tarana, I used to work here. I'm with Ntozake." It was *so good*. I went backstage with Ntozake, Valerie Simpson, everyone. Ntozake said, "I want to shout out the people who put this show on," and they gave us a standing ovation. It was a beautiful night.

But 2014 still ended up being one of the roughest years of my life. I was scared. So many people were collecting unemployment benefits at the time. It was like, "Oh, my unemployment ran out, let me extend it for another year." My payments started in six month increments, but I thought, no big deal, I'll just extend it if I need to. [But in December 2013, Congress declined to renew a jobless emergency aid program.] So, I only got unemployment for six months.

Going from getting fired to launching #MeToo was such a struggle. I wanted to lean in to the work I'd been doing, but I was doing it for free. We'd been trying to get a contract with the school we were working with. What being unemployed did, though, was make me go to the school and say, "We gotta get paid."

Then something else happened. I had met [film director] Ava DuVernay in Philly in 2010 when I was working at Art Sanctuary and she was working on her first film, *I Will Follow*. In 2014, when Ava got the job directing *Selma*, somebody reconnected us.

We talked and I was like, "Yeah, I'm deeply embedded in Selma [Burke moved to Selma in the late '90s after graduating from Alabama State University]; I'd love to help." The conversations turned into more emails, and then one day she asked me to come to Atlanta where they were filming. In Atlanta, I met her partner. He said, "We are putting you on payroll. You have to be a consultant on the film." And I was like, "Me?!"

I don't know if Ava ever really understood that hiring me on that film saved my life. I had zero dollars. The money she paid me got me through the summer and into the fall. I literally didn't know what I was going to do. My arts background and my work in Selma came back together and held me down because, baby, I was toast.

I'd started to feel like something might be possible. I went back to the schools I was working with and got a contract. I got a job at AFSC (American Friends Service Committee) at the end of 2015. I never chose jobs because "Oh, I need a job," but I needed to find something in social justice that paid. I moved to New York to work with Girls for Gender Equity (GGE)—a place where I could grow this work. I was figuring out my path.

Once I got my bearings, I kept thinking, "You've been carrying other people's visions to fruition for too long." The cloud a job can create over your eyes is so drastic. Being fired opened up possibilities for me. As soon as one thing breaks, everything else is open. It wasn't just the job. It's like: Should I be dating this guy? Should I cut my hair? So many things were called into question. Before, I wasn't asking the right questions. Maybe I would have come to similar conclusions, but how much longer would it have taken?

What I Learned

I think things happen when they're supposed to, in a way they're supposed to. Because I had that experience at Art Sanctuary, I was clear about my vision. That said, when I started #MeToo, I worried about what a heavy lift it would be to fully run an organization. But if I was gonna struggle underneath the thumb of anything—fundraising and schmoozing and doing all the things—it should be for my own thing. After twenty-five years, it was time.

I don't think we ever lose anything without gaining something. Also, these jobs aren't ours. We get so wrapped up in them that they feel like we own them, but we overestimate our importance. We're highly replaceable.

And this is not to say that everybody is an entrepreneur. Not everybody's going to start their own thing, get an LLC. It's perfectly fine if you get fired and get another job working for someone else. The job that is right for you. I think that things happen for a reason. At least, that's been true for most of my life, even in times that feel horrible and devastating.

What I would say is give yourself time to mourn the loss of that job. Feel all the feelings; they are valid. Do some self-reflection because maybe you deserved to be fired. Because not everybody's perfect. Maybe you took seventeen coffee breaks when you shouldn't have. There should be deep self-reflection. Loss begets growth. We just keep going to the next level—there's literally always something else. And don't let grass grow under your feet; you have to figure out what that something else is.

But I also think there's a culture of expediency. There's nothing wrong with being asked, "What's next?" and not knowing. We need to have a sense of self and grounded-ness and be like, "I don't know." Because most of the time, we don't.

Or, God forbid, you could say, "I'm sitting still. I'm so overwhelmed by what just happened to me. I think I need a minute. You'll be the first to know." Like, mind your business. Give me a chance to breathe. We are not identified by what we do in the world.

We have to figure out how, as a society, we can have grace for people and untether ourselves from this urgency of knowing what people are doing all the time. So much of that is insecurity, right? "Are you OK? *Am I OK?*" It's a circle jerk of insecurity.

Sit down, get your chi together, take some deep breaths, and lay off the lattes. We need to find grace with each other.

Jamie Lee Curtis

Jamie Lee Curtis is an Oscar-winning actress. She was fired from the TV series *Operation Petticoat* in 1977.

"My firing gave me tremendous insecurity... But once I got fired I got the opportunity to audition for *Halloween*, an opportunity that determined the rest of my life."

I think being fired is one of everyone's greatest fears, right? It's universal. There's not an actor I know who doesn't feel this way, and in show business, there are plenty of stories to support that. It's an unspoken vulnerability. As actors, I think we're all a little terrified.

I am an untrained actor—not unprepared, because I'm very prepared when I work—but I'm an accidental actor. I went to the same college as my mother [Janet Leigh]. She was the most famous person who had attended, so she had a big legacy there. I had a D-plus average in high school, and like an 840 SAT score, *combined*. I had no business being in college.

I came home from college for Christmas break one year, and I ran into a man who used to teach tennis at my friend's tennis court in Beverly Hills. His name was Chuck Binder. He goes, "Hey, Jamie, I'm managing actresses now." (That's the story of Los Angeles: you're a coach, but you're now managing actors.) And I was like, "Oh, cool." He said, "They're looking for Nancy Drew at Universal, you should go up for it." Now, I had brown hair, and I was cute, so I was like, "OK." So, I went and auditioned for the role of Nancy Drew.

I didn't get the part, but when I left, they called him and said something like, "She's not going to get that part, but she was good." He told me, "You should stick around. You could be an actress."

I was like, no, no, no. But back in college, I was taking Intro to Drama, and I called the head of the department and asked if it was possible that if I stayed in LA, went to acting class, dance class, and auditions, could I write a paper and get credit for one semester talking about my experience trying to break into show business? He said yes.

So, I stayed in LA. I went on a lot of auditions, which I didn't land. One day Chuck said, "There's this contract program at Universal. They've seen your picture, and they would like you to come in and audition." I did a scene from the play *Butterflies Are Free*.

Universal was the only studio that still operated a studio system, where an actor auditioned and became part of a studio's talent pool, a "contract player." You were paid a nominal amount of money to keep you under contract, and the studio would assign you jobs on their productions.

I was offered a contract and quit college immediately. I wasn't getting paid a lot of money, but it was enough to live in an apartment in Studio City, and it had a little bit of job security (although the contracts were up every six months). You would sign a seven-year contract with six-month options to renew.

I was assigned a bunch of little episodic things: *Quincy*, *Emergency*, a lesbian biker in *The Hardy Boys/Nancy Drew Mysteries*, a grumpy waitress in the season opener of *Columbo*.

What Happened

There was a TV movie they were making, a remake of a movie my dad [Tony Curtis] had starred in, called *Operation Petticoat*. It was a World War II comedy that he starred in with Cary Grant where a navy submarine in the middle of the South Pacific is painted pink. (Tony's character was a shyster who bought cheap paint and turned it pink.) The premise of the movie was that they're sent to pick up five army nurses who are stranded in the middle of the war, and they have to board the submarine.

I was called to audition. I'm sure that every time a contract player auditioned for something, there was a little asterisk right next to your name, which meant they could pay you less. Lo and behold, I got cast as one of the nurses, to play the part opposite my dad's former role. I'm sure they thought that was cute.

We were halfway through shooting when the producers came to the set. They said, "ABC loves the footage, and they have picked up *Operation Petticoat* to be a half-hour single-camera comedy series starting this fall on ABC, and you're now all series regulars!"

We did all of the promos, the upfronts, the magazines—I mean, we were in *TV Guide*. I'm eighteen years old, and I'm the *female lead* of a TV series. It was a big deal.

That said, it was a half-hour show set on a submarine with five army nurses and eleven men. That's *sixteen* regulars. So, every time we would get a script, we would race through it and see how many lines each of us had.

We made it through one season with meh reviews, meh ratings. One day I was called to lunch at the commissary at Universal Studios with Ms. James [Monique James, who ran the contract department]. She said to me, "I have bad news. You've been fired. The truth is, they've let go of almost the entire cast of sixteen actors."

I immediately thought, *Oh fuck, that's it*. They're not going to pick up my [contract player] option. I'm going to lose my $235 a week, and I'm going to have to go back to college. I'm not going to be able to pay my rent. I was terrified.

I was embarrassed and a little humiliated, and I felt that sting of the adrenaline hit, the shame that someone was looking at me like, "You're not good enough." You know that awful feeling. And for sure I thought I was going to lose my contract, my paycheck, and I was going to have to move back in with my parents. All of a sudden, I was just going to be a hustling actor. I literally thought, "This is it. It's over."

Now, there are too many people who've gone through this, and certainly people with way rougher stories than mine. But it was real. I was fired from a TV series by a network for a studio who employed me, so, I thought that made me unemployable.

That day I was panicking driving home. I knew it was unlikely they were going to pick up my option. I'm sure I was sobbing.

What Next

A week or two later, Chuck sent me for an audition for this little movie that was being made in Hollywood by John Carpenter, *Halloween*. A horror movie. I auditioned many times and ultimately got the lead part of Laurie Strode. And I am sure having the daughter of the woman who starred in *Psycho* star in this film would be a little bit of a curio, a tiny frisson.

Halloween was my first job after *Operation Petticoat*, so there were some residual feelings there. I remember every second of the first day of work, from where I parked to how I felt. That evening I got home to my house in the Valley, where I lived with my roommate. The phone rang (you know, when you had one phone, and it was in the living room?). My roommate said, "Hey, Jamie, it's for you. It's John Carpenter," as she covered the phone with her hand. I remember the amount of time it took me to walk to that phone, ten feet that took what seemed like four hours. I let out a breath and said, "Hello?"

He said, "Hey, darlin', I just want you to know that you were fantastic today, and I'm so happy, and you were just wonderful, and it's going to be great. And I just wanted to tell you that."

That is the only time in my forty-five years of being a professional actor that anyone has ever called me after a first day of work and said, "I'm happy, good job." Because when you go home after your first day of work, you're filled with insecurity. I was very nervous that he was about to say to me, "Hey . . ." Because when they start with the word "Hey . . . ," in my experience it's usually an agent saying, "Hey . . . so," and then it's not good.

Halloween came out, but it took a few months before it started gaining a following. The only two jobs I got after *Halloween* came out were an episode of *The Love Boat*—where I'm in it with my mother—and a job on *Charlie's Angels*, where I played a professional golfer. That was the extent of the work I got from being in that movie.

What happened next, though, was that John Carpenter and Deborah Hill [*Halloween*'s producer] wrote a part in the movie *The Fog* for me. They felt bad that they'd eventually had big success from the movie as filmmakers and I hadn't had the same experience as an actor, as in no one was really casting me. So, then I did *The Fog*, and I became an actress. I was now hirable.

What I Learned

There's a quote I refer to all the time, from a novel called *Special Topics in Calamity Physics*, by Marisha Pessl. In the middle, there's a little op-ed that says most people think their life is based on their first job, where they went to college, what their starting salary was, who they marry, and that's how life sort of proceeds.

Instead, she writes, "... life hinges on a couple of seconds you never see coming. And what you decide in those few seconds determines everything from then on ... And you have no idea what you'll do until you're there."

I recently got an honorary doctorate in fine arts from the American Film Institute. And when I received my doctorate, I read this to the student body:

"You can plan all you want, but your life is going to hinge on a couple seconds you never see coming. What you do in that moment of crisis, in that moment of hinging, that's going to determine the rest of your life. And you're not going to know what you'll do until that happens. You can't plan for that moment."

Now, I'm not going to lie to you and say that getting fired from *Operation Petticoat* gave me a fire in my belly, and I was *going to show them*. That's not at all what happened. The truth is, my firing gave me tremendous insecurity. But by accident, the couple seconds I never saw coming was getting fired from that TV show.

But had I stayed on *Operation Petticoat* (which was, by the way, canceled two episodes into the next season), I would have missed the boat with *Halloween* [now, a near-fifty-year-old horror movie phenomenon, including thirteen films, video games, comic books, and Michael Myers masks]. I would have missed what became my lifelong trajectory, attached to a pumpkin, for forty-five years.

It's less about what being fired did to me personally. What it really did is make me realize that I have to put myself in the path of things. My phrase is always, "Suit up, show up. Arrive early, stay late. Be 150 percent, 200 percent prepared," so you can never be called out for not being prepared, which is a criterion for firing. This philosophy has served me well.

Acting is a business filled with rejection. And it's not just getting the job; it's when the job comes out. Filmmakers bring a piece of creativity into the world, it's then adjudicated, shat on most of the time, and judged harshly. And then *you're* judged harshly based on it.

When I won an Oscar in 2023 for *Everything, Everywhere, All at Once*—which was very surprising to me—I wanted in that moment of shock and awe to acknowledge the fact that I was in a genre of movies during my career that was not well regarded. They called them B movies. They literally reduced their value, like a restaurant grade. Like, do you get sushi from a restaurant that has a B?

I was part of a whole industry in show business—or show-off business, as I like to refer to it—that has a downgraded level of acceptance and respect. It was very important that on Oscar night, I was able to say to the audiences that had given me a career that this wasn't just me in *this* moment. This was me way, way back.

So, yes, life hinges on a couple seconds you may not see coming. For me, being fired was a moment of true shock and awe, and I didn't know at the time that it was better for me to have gotten fired. Even though I went through all the shame and the self-doubt and the insecurity that went along with it, what came from it, in my lucky circumstances, was a movie that then ended up being something.

Those seconds, whatever they were, led to something I never imagined in my life. *Everything, Everywhere, All at Once.*

12

Managing Your Exit and Networking

Master Your Messaging and Utilize Your Connections

The best part about getting fired, quite honestly, is reading all the beautiful eulogies about yourself (texts from friends, DMs from colleagues and strangers), but *you're still alive*. It's kinda... great? If you'd just "left" your job, that doesn't happen so much. The message that Laura values most? An Instagram DM from a sixty-something-year-old lady from Mississippi named Boo that read, "Laura, I only ever read magazines that you worked for. Thank you for making me feel included." Kristina was grateful for the friend who commented on her Instagram about her editorial vision but also for saying she remained "a lovely human throughout." And another, with a dash more sarcasm: "Thanks for providing my exact unsubscribe date."

After that wave of communication is over, you'll *finally* have the time to think deeply about what makes you happy and unhappy in your professional life. Like we said earlier about thinking like a kid, *we all* have the ability to review what makes us happy, challenged, and fulfilled versus, well, what makes us feel like crap. Now you have time to "edit" your professional priorities: that metaphorical red pencil will not only remind you of what you love, but refresh your energy and focus.

Here's the key: If you've done great work and built a solid reputation, you'll be pleasantly reminded of that by the people who show up for you. And you have every right to reach out to the contacts you have made—and earned—over the years. Do a "fired tour" in person and on Zoom. Also, embrace the unexpected; get out of your lane and look at broader opportunities. You'll be surprised what bubbles up: explore it.

Oh, and you know how we've said *own your firing*? Well, it bears repeating, do *not* agree to the great cover-up! The old "We'll follow your narrative" (code for lying about it) is another example of the bizarro-coded language around firing. While it might seem like the easy way out—an elegant, mutual "parting of ways"—it's actually a trap. The more you spin, evade, and try to "PR" your exit, the lonelier and more fraudulent you will feel. It's such a waste of energy trying to contrive anything but the truth, energy that you dearly need to reboot your system and your well-being.

Here's the thing: the truth is not shameful. It's freeing! There's real power in being able to say, "Yeah, I got fired." When you own it, you strip away the stigma. It becomes part of your story—not the defining chapter, but rather a page in it that says, "I'm resilient, and I'm moving on." And here's the kicker: more people respect honesty than infallibility.

You can also take it a step further and post the news on social media. Laura posted a video on Instagram saying "Fuck 'em" and taking a tequila shot with the *InStyle* team, but she most certainly does not recommend that for everyone. After taking a day to pack up her office (how did she have twelve coats?!), she also took a "fired portrait" outside the DotDash Meredith building, but instead of the traditional box with a sad potted plant (she hadn't been in the office for over a year because of Covid), she posed with her office mascot, Norman, a giant stuffed koala (below).

Kristina was fired in late April but didn't officially leave until mid-June. In the twenty-four hours between learning the news and the press reporting it, she sent short notes of gratitude to her most loyal supporters so that they heard it from her first. From the beginning, she opted for transparency—the only version of the story she wanted out there was the truth. (Why spin when you're already spinning out?)

Her boss gave the expected speech to the team: ye olde "Thanks for all you've done, but we're going in a different direction." Like Laura, Kristina also threw down some company-funded tequila—because if there ever was a moment for it, this was it.

For her own farewell speech, Kristina was inspired by a *WSJ. Magazine* column from 2015 on "Luck" (featuring wisdom from one Tom Selleck) she found while cleaning out her desk:

"You know, Tom Selleck was right," she told her team. "He said: 'The closer you get to being lucky, the bigger the disappointments will be when you're not.'"

After that, the six weeks from the firing to Kristina's last day felt oddly liberating—freedom wrapped in a lame duck label. She packed up her office at her own pace, tied up loose ends, downloaded her contacts, and wrote her final Editor's Letter. She also took time to craft a note to her staff that recapped all their accomplishments (this is important because it's shareable and also a canny move to have a list of your successes out in the world).

Laura insisted Kristina capture the dwindling days at her desk with her own "sad fired photo" (on the previous page) that includes boxes and boxes of books and her desk ephemera jammed into FreshDirect bags. [Note from Laura: it didn't look all that sad because Kristina's hair is so good.] But already, this book was brewing.

As a parting gift, Kristina's team presented her with a beautiful volume filled with personal messages. It took a few months before she could gather the strength to read them. It was hard; they made her cry. But they also reminded her of the lasting impact she'd made and reaffirmed her desire to own her narrative.

Kristina left with her dignity and sense of self intact—and resolved to turn this professional setback into something greater.

In short, you want to handle your exit as elegantly as possible. While it may not feel like it, in the end, this will serve you. Again, this doesn't mean spinning it, just communicating what happened with grace. And as much as you might want to publicly screw the bastards—well, don't.

Craft an "I Got Laid Off" Announcement

In the least expected, most surprising way, you can turn your firing into a moment. "It's worthwhile for you to write a very even, constructive social post saying, 'Hey, this thing happened,' because those posts get a lot of traction," says career coach Phoebe Gavin. "People see them and want to support the person. Sometimes it can be complete strangers who will reach out and be helpful in some way."

Gavin speaks from experience. "That was the case in my most recent layoff. I posted, 'I just got laid off, this is how I think about it.' And I got a lot of really great feedback and interest from people in my professional network and people who saw my tweet who were willing to help." That said, Gavin recommends another set of eyes to review your post before posting. "It's not something you should do on your own. Get some help from somebody who has more perspective on the situation unless you are really, really good at controlling your emotions under duress."

And get that—tight!—statement out *fast*: "Like the day of or day after, so you can leverage all the activity that [comes your] way," says Optima Careers' Marianne Ruggiero. "You need an exit statement that works. It doesn't have to be long, three or four sentences that answer the basic questions people will want to ask."

"A statement might say, 'Hi friends. I've just wrapped up five successful years at X company. Here were my achievements. I'm in the market for my next role. I'd love to reconnect with any of my former colleagues. Please reach out anytime. I'd love to get coffee,'" says executive recruiter Kristy Hurt. "That can get conversations going. It's important to be really active in all of your social networks and not just disappear into a black hole. It's good to process information and put yourself out there. Don't dwell on the bad news."

But again, be clear and don't beg questions. "If you just say, 'My job was eliminated,' then I sit there and say, 'Well, why was your job eliminated instead of somebody else's?'" says Ruggiero. If it was a wider company thing, be sure to include that.

Super importantly, if your company is releasing a statement, ask to be part of that process: "It's really maintaining the executive skill set of communicating the right way," says HR expert Bucky Keady. "Insist on being a part of the communication. Because that communication can go haywire."

LinkedIn career expert Catherine Fisher says, "What you don't want to do is complain like, 'I just got fired, and I hate this company, working here was terrible.' That's not going to do you any favors. Instead, signal to your community that, yes, you're open to work.

"So, if you're going on LinkedIn and sharing that you lost your job—you can choose how much you want to share in that regard—add the types of roles that you're looking for, if anyone in your network is looking for these types of skills. Be specific about what you need from people; that's how you'll get the most out of it."

And while you're surely feeling low, try not to sink. Hurt says, "A lot of people are filled with so much shame that they don't say anything and just kind of go into this reclusive 'I hate myself, I'm terrible at everything' headspace. Try not to do that because people want to work with people who are engaged, excited, trying new things, exploring new opportunities. All of this is so appealing, and you never know what could be around the corner."

Be Strategic About Social Media

You don't have to be blasting about your work situation on LinkedIn, Instagram, X, Threads, TikTok, Snapchat . . . oh, hi, Bluesky! If you're all over everything, you'll likely look defensive and a little deranged. Identify the platform most used by the industry you're in or want to join (corporate or creative, say), and read the room. Do your research: pay attention to what people you admire post and how often they do it. A good rule of thumb is to post only when you have something notable to say, or if you want to strategically comment on someone else's post. As the old fashion adage goes, "Less is more."

Lorraine K. Lee, an instructor at Stanford Continuing Studies and LinkedIn Learning, says, "The way most people learn about you first is online instead of face-to-face. So, your presence in terms of where you are appearing, where people are finding you, is really key."

Marketing expert Sylvia Long-Tolbert recommends, "Make a strategic decision. You have to be really careful with selecting platforms and what you can readily manage. That means keeping it up-to-date, keeping a pulse on the analytics—who comes, how often they come—what content about you are they finding useful? Being anywhere and everywhere without an active and updated voice isn't helpful."

"Boosting your brand is probably like any other intentional sales pitch," Long-Tolbert adds. This is where it pays, again, to think like an editor—or a composer, even. Yes, you are promoting yourself, but be conscious of your messaging, rhythm, and pacing. "Many people are turned off if you post a stream of consciousness," she says. "Most of my posts are about my craft—maybe 15 percent are about my greatness. You have to strike that balance."

Don't Go Scorched Earth on the Internet

While it might feel good in the moment to write a Substack screed about your former bosses (or film one of those viral getting-fired TikToks), life is not a movie and social media posts are just one screen grab away from immortality. Do you want one rant to define you? Nope. And why give your former bosses the time and energy anyway—you don't even *go there* anymore.

Gavin says, "Scorched earth social media posts and people

posting their layoffs on TikTok are probably very cathartic, getting something off your chest, but they ultimately don't work toward getting you to that next chapter. It may even make it harder."

And keep it together in your HR layoff meeting, too—even if you might be plotting recourse later. Kristy Hurt says, "You want to be able to leave with grace and not burn your bridges, because you want to be able to leave with a positive reputation. You want those HR people to recommend you wholeheartedly for the next thing. And if you blow up in the moment and say something that you might regret, it won't be good for you in the long run."

Bucky Keady agrees: "I don't advise vomiting forth everything. You have a reputation. You're going to be in a job again, at some point."

Know Everyone's Going to Call You

All sorts of people will get in touch—from the curious to the gossipy, from the pragmatic to the "Let me know what I can do for you" generous. You might be in the fetal position, but take these calls and talk it out. These people are thinking of you, and that alone should make you feel better. You'll start seeing that there's a road beyond what you thought was a dead end.

The New York Times Your Money columnist Ron Lieber says, "There are all sorts of rewards to being a good person. If you are a person who has thrown the rope back—reached out when others have had the same thing happen to them—that is going to come back to you in a tidal wave." You may feel overwhelmed, but take in what they have to say, digest it, and get back to them.

"You may not actually be prepared for it," adds Lieber, "and yet you're going to want to take advantage of it." He recommends thinking about it in the same way you would script a post on social media. "You want to have an answer to the question that people are going to ask, which is, 'How can I help?'"

Lieber also recommends filling your calendar, and fast. It will give you a sense of purpose; that feeling of busyness that you've just lost from your day-to-day. "Say to people, 'Take me to lunch in six weeks so that I can spend half an hour telling you about all the things I'm thinking about.' Put the lunch on the calendar, put the drink on the calendar, put the breakfast on the calendar, put the coffee on the calendar. You could do more than one a day. You're going to have time now."

At your meetings, Hurt says, "Ask for what you need and be clear about what you want. Being able to articulate it is important because if you can't tell them exactly what you're looking for, they're not really going to be able to help you."

Again, even if your mind is a little scrambled, don't wait. People are offering to help you *now*. So, put that help in your schedule. Unlike all the meetings and obligations in your previous job, these meetings are about *you*. That will motivate you and give you some focus. Be excited about that because it's . . . exciting!

But Also, Call Everyone

You'll likely be surprised by just how many contacts and allies you've made during your career—be it your first job or twenty years in. Of course, it's prudent to make deliberate connections that will help you in your industry, but often the greatest relationships are the ones you've made organically. Your pal from the coffee room, a partner on a project, people you bonded with at drinks in the bar by your office. So, if they haven't called you already (sometimes people get nervous and don't know what to say), reach out to them.

Don't be scared to do it: remember, the worst thing that could happen... already did. "Most people hate this advice because they feel more self-conscious about reaching out to people they already know than reaching out to brand-new people," says Gavin. "But people who already know you, especially if they've worked with you in the past, are invested in you in some way. They want you to be successful."

Ruggiero adds, "People think that you network to get the job. I would argue that you network to do a good job, to be a higher performer and to be known in the market, so when there are opportunities, they find you."

Get in Touch with Your Former Colleagues

Again, it's not weird! So, don't make it weird. Just because you were let go from the company and your work pals weren't doesn't mean they never want to talk to you again. In fact, they probably feel bad and will want to help you get back on your feet.

Gavin advises, "Reach out to the folks you were closest to who may still be at the company and ask them if they would be comfortable helping you find your next role. Depending on where they are in the organization, they can help in different ways. It could just be commiseration. If it's someone in a leadership position, perhaps they can look at your LinkedIn, résumé, or cover letter and give you leads."

A reminder: don't overthink it. These people know you, so you have a shorthand. Just say hi and that you'd love to catch up. They know what it's about. "You already worked with them for years," says Gavin. "You don't need to write some Shakespearean LinkedIn message."

Speaking of LinkedIn, the site says, "LinkedIn data finds that you're more likely to get hired through someone in your network than through a cold application. So, make sure you're tapping into your network to find connections who can help make an introduction to a hiring manager or connect you with someone who works at a company you're interested in."

Isn't that ironic, data telling you that human connections are best? We told you!

Ask for Introductions

"So many jobs are given to people, or people learn about jobs, through people they know and trust," says Hurt. "It's not cold networking, it's, 'Oh, I'm really close with this person who's besties with this person. You guys will love each other.' Having someone in common to endorse you can lead to opportunities that often don't even get posted to the outside world."

And don't just blurt out, "I need a job!" (Which you probably wouldn't, unless you've been drinking.) Take it down a notch and just meet, meet, meet. Jill Mizrachy, group people lead at Booz Allen Hamilton, says, "You can leverage a small group of people to start a network that will grow exponentially if you keep the door open. The minute you ask the question, 'I'm looking for a job. Do you have an opportunity?' you have literally closed the door. The next time you want to call that person, they're going to go, 'Oh God. She's calling me again for a job.'"

Business is like dating: it's not cute to keep calling (and if you have a bad time, don't go back). "As long as you keep the conversation open and positive, they will leverage their network, maybe even extend themselves to you, invite you to come back and check in. You're going to keep those lines of communication open and robust," Mizrachy says.

If You Were Laid Off in a Group, Start a Group Chat

"Create a cohort of the folks who were laid off, especially if there are some similarities in terms of your functions, because you can help each other—at the very least from a mental health perspective. Like *ah, this sucks* together versus it sucking alone," says Gavin. "You can pass leads on to each other. You can talk about what you're experiencing and what you're seeing, and that could be really helpful. And then once one person lands, sometimes they can help other people land in that same company."

Laura did this exact thing with her *InStyle* team, relishing her side hustle as a part-time HR department. Seeing and helping her previous colleagues land in new roles—some even starting their own businesses—after such an upset for them was hugely gratifying. At Sotheby's, one of Kristina's first moves was to bring on two women who had been casualties of her departure at *WSJ*.

Dominique Browning

Dominique Browning is the director and co-founder of Moms Clean Air Force and an author. She was fired from her position as editor in chief of *House & Garden* in 2007.

"The shame game is of little use."

What Happened

I had absolutely no idea it was coming. I was told, "We're not going to go further with this magazine. We're closing it." So, that was it.

The entire time I was there [1995–2007], there were rumors that I was about to get fired or that the magazine was about to close. It was constant. But that's pretty much life at Condé Nast.

I came from the outside: news media and education. I certainly had never been in the shelter [magazine] world and so, you know, I was kind of an easy target in many ways. But then these macroeconomic issues started to take hold [the run-up to the Great Recession of 2008]—you really felt it in the housing sector almost immediately. So, I was sort of on the cutting edge of the entire magazine business starting to slide, from which it has not emerged nor recovered.

Every time I had a great publisher and we would start to really hit our stride, they would say, "Oh, we could use that person at *The New Yorker*. We want that person for *Condé Nast Traveler*." There was so much chaos. Every time a publisher leaves, they take their ad director, they take their marketing people, and every new kid comes in and is like, "Oh, what's the mission?" It was a lot of turmoil, much more than any organization can bear. I just said, "Let's just do the best possible magazine we can do and let the magazine speak for itself." Readers loved it. Renewal rates were fantastic. As were the rest of the numbers I had any control over.

After it happened, so many people said to me, "You didn't get fired; they closed the magazine," and I said, "No, I got fired." And what's worse is *everybody* got fired. I knew who had mortgages and what kind of financial burdens people had. I knew who was getting divorced. I knew everything. Including the kind of impact it would have. And it was devastating.

I was despondent; I was deranged. Over the next few months, I would get out of the subway in Midtown and look around and think, "Where am I?" I would go in and out of these episodes. I remember I passed a gym that was having a big sale and thought the sign said "Mommy Back Guarantee." And I thought, "Oh, my mommy will come back and she will save me." And then I realized it said "Money Back Guarantee."

Some people said that because I had savings, I had no right to feel bad. But money was a deep fear. I had saved money, but I also had real estate that I had to sell because if there was one huge, massive storm, my house could be in the water. I thought, "I can't have my life savings go floating away."

Work was my identity, and it was a badge of honor. I was born in 1955, and I have worked since I was a teenager. Why did I feel like I needed to work all the time? It was a real feminist thing. I did not want to be supported by a man. I didn't want my father to support me. It just felt like I needed to work.

Eventually, I decided I better just start doing things. But it took *many, many* months. I began writing as a form of self-therapy. That narrative I had written for myself became my book *Slow Love: How I Lost My Job, Put on My Pajamas, and Found Happiness*.

By the time the book came out in 2010, I still didn't know where things were going to go. But my theme and my mantra became "Just Say Yes." To anybody who calls you, to anytime anybody wants you to do something—*just say yes*. I thought maybe the thing I say yes to will turn into something else. At the time, I thought it would be another magazine. But the further away I got from it, the more I started thinking: "Why do I want to go back and do what I've always done? Maybe this is a moment to think completely creatively and just reinvent myself."

What Next

Saying yes was a really good exercise because I got some consulting gigs and did some work for *The Wall Street Journal*. One day I had lunch with a friend of a friend who was on the board of the Environmental Defense Fund [EDF]. She said she used to love my Editor's Letters and my essays. She suggested I write about what the Environmental Defense Fund does, because they had a hard time explaining it. And so, I said yes.

I started interviewing people and writing a column for the EDF. It was nothing like *House & Garden*. I did interviews with scientists and economists and policy writers, and I would get to the end of a forty-five-minute discussion—and I would call myself an intelligent, educated person—and I'd say, I don't understand a word you just said. Start over. And now you need to tell me what you do in a language that your mother could understand. That's when I realized they had a big communication problem there.

I was also meeting with headhunters in the nonprofit world. I thought, "I have a lot to bring to this picture. I know how to communicate. I know marketing." But I was told, "You don't know anything about the nonprofit world. We're not interested in you. It doesn't translate." So, I thought, "OK, that means I have to figure out how to do this a different way."

This was thirteen or fourteen years ago. The entire green advocacy movement was in a depression, and it looked like nothing was going to happen. And that's when I realized one of the problems was that nobody was talking to voters. At the same time, I had started blogging (remember blogging?) in anticipation of my book coming out. At the time, there were all these women who were self-described mommy bloggers, and I started looking at that because it was really interesting to me. And what were they writing about? How do we protect our children? What do we need to buy that's toxin and chemical free? I'm reading all this and thinking, "How can we harness all of that energy toward the climate movement?" And that's how Moms Clean Air Force was born.

During an interview I was doing for my book, I met an older woman. She was very wise. She said to me, "Honey, go where the love is. You gotta go where the love is." At the time, I said, "Oh, yeah, that's nice." I didn't really know what she meant.

But a year later, there I was thinking I *love* talking to these scientists. I love the idea that I can take care of my children, even though they no longer need me to take care of them, but I can be thinking about the world my children will inherit. Maybe this is where the love is; maybe this is what I need to be doing.

Getting to this place was its own adventure. Now, I work with about twenty people and we have a website that is full of news and information and resources and we have 1.5 million members all over the country. All my previous media work allowed me to help communicate to people why they need to care about these issues. I do a lot of writing about climate and mental-health issues. Another group of people work on regulation and laws, and so we spend tons of time in Washington. We testify in front of the Environmental Protection Agency; we demand stronger laws. We are trying to change things on a systemic level.

A lot of the work we do is hearing people's stories about what they've gone through. We find people who will testify in front of

Congress or the EPA. The most gratifying part is when we convince legislators or the EPA that we need stronger regulations for X or Y and then it happens—I can say I brought three hundred moms to testify in front of the EPA three hundred times. My day-to-day work is just like what I did as an editor in chief—working with people who have different skills and deploying them.

What I Learned

I never thought I would get fired because I am such a hard worker. But it happened, and so it could happen again, right? I don't think that feeling ever goes away. But being fired made me realize, "OK, my resilience muscle is back; it's working. It's not gonna be the end of the world."

I tell people, "Give yourself permission to mourn." I loved the magazine world, and I loved the luxury world. I loved all of it. I loved fashion. I loved, *love*, all of that. It was more I just felt like I'm done with that, you know, I'm done. It was liberating.

I felt there was real virtue and value in doing what we did with magazines. So many of us got our news and our information from magazines. Even when we were talking about celebrities and fashion, we were also talking about what people were doing to make the world better. What I'm doing now is that, but in a different way.

After losing my job, I felt like I had to get over my guilt, over feeling bad. But it's important to just let yourself mourn because you are mourning work that you were passionate about, a project that you loved doing with people who were like your family. In the days before remote work, I spent more time with my colleagues than with my children.

Women are capable of carrying a lot of shame. But the shame game is of little use. Like I said, people tried to tell me I wasn't fired. They didn't even want to hear me say it. But I think if you don't call it what it is, it's very hard to get past it, and it's also hard to say to yourself, "What *did* go wrong here?" I was loyal to a fault and kept thinking, "I gotta keep doing this because, otherwise, we're totally destabilized." I should have left years earlier.

Mika Brzezinski

Mika Brzezinski is the co-anchor of MSNBC's *Morning Joe* and founder of Know Your Value. She was fired from her role as a CBS News correspondent in 2006.

"Being fired took away the poser in me."

What Happened

I was about to replace John Roberts as the CBS weekend news anchor, but then everything blew up during the Memogate scandal [when Dan Rather cited fake documents in a *60 Minutes* segment about President George W. Bush's service with the Texas Air National Guard]. Dan Rather ended up stepping down from *CBS Evening News*. Days before I was fired, CBS hired Katie Couric to be the main anchor. Remember, back then, a woman anchor was groundbreaking for the evening news. And then, on the weekend, to have *another* woman? It was too much.

I spent a long time thinking, "What was it? What was it about me they didn't like?" When men are fired, they're like, "Screw them. It's not me. It's them." And women immediately go, "It's me." I thought about this for a year. I wasted so much time and had a lot of terrible interviews where you could see my consternation written all over my face.

The day I was let go, as I walked out of CBS and along 57th Street, I just remember being in shock. I loved my job. I had balanced work and family (I brought my kids to work with me). I'd really figured it out. So, having to leave this all behind, I was heartbroken.

I remember calling my dad, who always answered the phone on the first ring when I was in distress. It's a weird kind of telepathic connection that we had. When I called to tell him I was getting divorced; when I called to tell him I was fired; when I called with some mental-health struggles after 9/11.

Sure enough, he picked up, and that made me start crying, immediately. I was almost forty years old, and I was weeping like a ten-year-old who'd gotten in big trouble at school. He was so sweet. He talked about disappointment. "You'll see in the long run. It'll be the best thing that ever happened to you." He asked for more details and said, "Wow, their loss."

But I just couldn't see it that way. I told my husband; he totally understood and was on my side. That said, I put on a ridiculous dog-and-pony show for my kids. I lied. I was wiping tears off my face and was like, "Girls, I'm going to be able to spend more time with you!" And they were like, "Huh?"

My daughter Carlie is very empathic; she knew something was wrong. And my older daughter, Emilie, was like, "What do you mean?"

I said, "I'm not going to be working at CBS anymore. I'm here to be with you, a stay-at-home mom. And it's going to be *great*," I lied.

She was like, "You can't do that. You can't leave CBS. That's the only reason the lady at the library likes me."

The next morning Carlie's teacher called me and said, "Could you come in? Carlie is really upset."

I said, "Sure I can, I'm a stay-at-home mom!" I race to school, and I see Carlie on the floor by the lockers.

The teacher says, "She just told me that you were going to be leaving your job."

I lean down and say, "Carlie, this is good news. I get to spend more time with you!"

And she looked up, her eyes full of tears, and she said, "Mommy, you can't leave CBS. You love it so much."

On the money front, I was really scared. My husband worked, but our combined salaries made it possible for us to live in a place where the school was great, and the girls were happy. I was worried about having to move and telling people who supported me and my family that I would no longer be able to support them. That was hard.

I would put the losing career status issue this way: At CBS, one of my favorite things was going on the road with the camera guys and the producers and being part of a team. The crew became your best friends, living with them in the foxhole that was covering a news story—people you shared life with. I had worked very hard to become a good, competent part of the team. They had taught me everything I knew, and I was grateful. Losing my job, I felt

I had disappointed them, and also kind of ostracized, honestly. It's as painful as being locked out of a middle school clique, but much worse, because you need it to survive, to thrive, to bring that dynamic home to your family.

I took it hard. I was completely deflated. It was invalidating to my kids, because I was trying to be so happy to be with them. And they could tell that work was something I needed and missed. I don't know why I didn't feel proud to say that. It felt untoward, almost.

During that year I did a lot of exercising, a lot of walks, which was sometimes hard when I was down. It was a difficult time, and I don't necessarily like the way I handled it. I didn't believe in myself, and people could see that. After all that work, I should have known my value. That's why I wrote the book *Know Your Value* [2011], which became a women's career platform. Because those feelings are so real when your stock is down. And you know who you need to depend on in those moments? You!

What Next

I was going crazy, not working for over a year. Because I had such a serious dysfunction in confidence, instead of looking for something comparable to the job I had, I called MSNBC and said, "I don't care what you think I want. I know you don't have an anchor or reporter position. What *do* you have? I'll do it."

They were like, "You're way overqualified."

I said, "No, I'm not. I'm not working right now, so I'd like to know what you have."

I took a job as a freelance newsreader (you sit there for eight hours and do two thirty-second news cut-ins). I was like, "I'm in." One, I needed to bring in money. Two, I needed to be working. We were so miserable. Our family Christmas card that year was Jim, me—with a bottle of vodka—and the girls have signs. One says, "Please Hire Her," and the other says, "Get Her Out of Here." At least we could laugh.

I got like a couple of hundred dollars a day, no benefits. On the first day I went back in and went *beep* with a pass that said "Mika" and "MSNBC." I was so happy.

Everyone was like, "Why did you take that job?" I didn't care. I was being useful. I was being productive. I was bringing in money. It was like 90 percent less than what I had made. But you know what? They started calling me every day. And they're like, "Hey, you're good. Can you fill-in host on our show?" Yes, I can.

This is what I tell anybody who has that feeling like, "I'm gone. I'm done. I'm spent. It's over." My skills and ability came back in *two seconds*. But it's because I took a massive step back. I could do the job with my hands tied behind my back. That was what I needed to develop confidence again.

Don't underestimate a job that's a step back. Don't turn your nose up at opportunity. Any opportunity is an opportunity, right? And that opportunity puts you in place for more opportunities.

Within three to four months, I was working seven days a week. Then in April 2007, Don Imus got kicked off the air (his CBS show was simulcast on MSNBC) and they were looking to start a morning show, *Morning Joe*, with one of their political hosts, Joe Scarborough. I was asked to fill in as host and try out for that. So, if I hadn't taken that step back, I wouldn't have been in place for the biggest move of my life—that I had no idea was yet to come.

[Filling in on *Morning Joe* in July later that year, Brzezinski ripped up a script on air in protest over the producers choosing a clickbait-y Paris Hilton story as lead news over a conflict in Iraq.] I was still freelance at that time. I think that script rip got me the hosting job. Well, I almost got fired again until they realized it could be a good thing.

Being fired took away the poser in me. I was no longer trying to fit the bill, I was in "Fuck it" mode. Honestly, after that, what could they do? Fire me? I'm going to be me. I know who I am after all of this—the great highs and the low lows—and all the things in between. It's called growing up.

What I Learned

One of the most important tenets of Know Your Value is getting through all of it psychologically. It *is* their loss. But what am I gaining from this experience? I need to power through, I need to dig deep, I need to figure out how to make money, I need to act quickly. And if you're struggling with the concept of getting fired and how to couch it—like I was with my kids—you lose your own plot. It's OK to say, "I got fired. I got canned."

There was not an event or cause that triggered my firing at CBS. They simply no longer needed my services anymore. But I loved it there. And I did such great work. I did a series on bipolar disorder and young children. I traveled the country. Do you see, by the way, how I've already turned the conversation to my great work? I would never criticize the place that I just left. That's an important message: You can trust me. I can handle something with dignity. I just said all those things and turned the conversation to my work in thirty seconds.

How to spin it is ... truthfully. You don't have to explain, but you need to manage the conversation. Use the conversation to talk about your strong points. If you feel you need to disparage your former employer, that's not going to work for you.

When I got fired, I documented my feelings because I knew feeling this bad about myself was wrong. I thought, if my confidence is so low, and I've had the blessing of an incredible education, of multilingual parents who are Eastern European refugees who've taught me so much—how is it for women who don't have access, who live in places that aren't close to resources? I need to give back when I figure this out. I coach women on communicating effectively. I love sharing my vulnerabilities because usually people are very surprised to hear that I have them, given what I project.

But when *Morning Joe* started, I struggled with renegotiating my own contract. I failed by accepting the first thing they offered. I was like, "Oh my God. Yes, I'm hired? Yes, I'm signing! I'm signing the contract!" (You would have thought it was my first job, ever.) You also need to know when your stock is up. After ripping up that script, my stock started soaring—but the only person who didn't see it was me.

I thought, "I'm going to share my process of renegotiating terribly and my part in equal pay that didn't go well." This is the part of the equation we can control. Let me study this, talk to women around the world, and build a platform where they can learn to know their value.

Know Your Value ended up being four books, a platform, and maybe twenty events across the US. It's led to the 50 Over 50 list, which is a partnership with *Forbes*, and now we have the *Forbes* 30/50 Summit in Abu Dhabi every International Women's Day. The summit takes women from the global 50 Over 50 list, women from *Forbes* 30 Under 30, and has a cross-cultural, generational, multilingual mentoring event. It is remarkable.

What would I say to my fired self now? "Oh my God, how wrong you were. Get over it and get on the phone. It is not a big deal. The only person making a big deal is you."

15

Getting Hired

Getting Yourself Out There to Get That Job

Now that you've redefined your new professional "era," it's time to go get that job. And, since Laura went on to start her own business, she's going to go send some emails while Kristina covers this chapter intro.

After Kristina's departure from *WSJ*, she was at a crossroads, deeply contemplating (code for overthinking) her next career move. With all due respect to the almost eight million freelance workers in the United States, she knew that the consulting hustle wasn't for her. Yet the search for what came next wasn't just about finding another job; it was about finding a position that could be as spiritually fulfilling as her last. (Lofty goals, for sure.) But with real-world obligations like rent and tuition for her two children square on her shoulders, those "soul goals" had to be paired with down-to-earth pragmatism.

Like a networking octopus, she spent the next six months taking every opportunity to connect: Zoom meetings, coffees, breakfasts, lunches, drinks, dinners, calls, texts, DMs, and even a quick trip for a meeting in Paris (it was for work!). She was searching for a role that resonated on multiple levels—fulfilling her aspirations, covering her financial needs, and sparking up her brain for new challenges. She was as close as she'll ever get to becoming a "manifester."

The CEO of Sotheby's, who had reached out to Kristina immediately after her layoff, had planted a seed early on. As time passed and she took *all the meetings*, the idea of launching a media division for the storied auction house was the thing that most excited her. What really appealed to Kristina was the opportunity to build something from scratch, within a historic company. She also knew that going in, she could set boundaries that would allow her time to write this book and shape her role on the board of the Swedish fashion brand Toteme. The idea of a broader professional life and a more balanced personal one? Well, that would be living the dream.

While Kristina's experience may not be universal, it offers lessons about how to navigate the job market more effectively. Namely, she took her time and didn't rush into anything. You need to make sure you're ready before you start interviewing. If you're still mentally scrambled from your layoff, take a beat. You don't want to be ricocheting around the job market like a nervous pinball. Booz Allen Hamilton's Jill Mizrachy advises, "The very first thing I tell people is *do not interview*. You're not in any condition to do it. There's nothing worse than trying to bounce back and immediately scramble to find a new job: 'I've *got* to be out there.' No, you don't. You will not put your best foot forward."

So, while you have this paranoid (but precious) time, sit down and think about who you want to be professionally, now that you have a little time to reboot. You'll be getting a new security badge and scanning that daily cafeteria menu before you know it.

Consider a Career Coach

A coach or consultant can be invaluable if: one, you've been in a job for years and have no idea how to make yourself marketable; two, you've lost confidence; or three, you're thinking about changing industries. They also will help you get out of your own head and become a "salable candidate," as they say in the biz. And that, as they used to say in the Mastercard ads, is priceless.

WSJ offered Kristina a coach as part of her "retraining allowance" (kind of reminds us of housebreaking puppies, but that's what they call it). Considering she had been in her role for over a decade and hadn't updated her résumé once in those ten years, there was a lot to update on LinkedIn, so she appreciated the structured time with the coach, getting unvarnished feedback on her accomplishments and positioning. After just two sessions, her bio was ready to post.

An Unbiased Opinion on Your Potential Next Steps

The most valuable thing a career coach can give you is a macro perspective on, well, your career. You are too close to it, as are your family and friends. Career coach Phoebe Gavin says, "Friends, family, or mentors in your current industry have a vested interest in the outcome. A career coach does not. I don't care what you do. I care if you're happy. But, say, your mom wants you to be a lawyer. Your boyfriend wants you to stay in New York. Your mentor doesn't think you should leave the industry at all. A lot of the noise embedded in advice you get from those close to you when you're making a career shift can either send you in the wrong direction or prevent you from taking action."

If You're Unmoored for Months and Need Centering

Gavin advises, "My rule of thumb is, if you've been trying to solve the problem yourself for a month or more and you have not made any progress, you need to try something different. And that different thing probably needs to be an expert." That expert doesn't need to be a career coach; it could just be someone else in your professional network.

"But once you get to the multiple month point and you still aren't progressing—you still aren't achieving your goals—that's when it makes sense for you to bite the bullet and work with an expert who can work directly with you. You are accountable to them, and if you're paying someone, even if it's a small amount of money, they're accountable to you. Then you can move forward."

What Does Career Coaching Cost?

Well, it depends. Fees differ widely depending on the job you are seeking (entry-level to C-Suite), whether you need in-person or remote advice, if you need one-on-one time, or whether you're happy to be part of a group coaching. Entry-level coaches range from $75–$150 per hour for private coaching, with high-profile executive coaching landing at $300 to $500-plus.*

Gavin explains, "There are lots of career coaches who offer multiple coaching formats. Most people come to career coaching and expect it to work like therapy, where you give me money and I give you an hour. Coaches don't have those constraints. We can be very flexible and inventive about the formats that we work in. I do thirty-minute sessions and sixty-minute sessions. I have an app that I talk to people in. I have a group coaching program at a much more accessible cost where people can hang out with me on a weekly basis."

Applying for Jobs

Tailor Your Résumé to Each Job You Apply For

You can't just copy-paste each job application—it looks lazy and insincere. Add a personal touch but make sure all the relevant keywords are there. "You have to customize your résumé for every single job you apply to," says Mizrachy. "If you're only applying electronically, 90 percent of big companies are using text

---

* The average hourly fee will differ according to where you are based, but it's wise to ask for recommendations first, and also ask a few coaches to get a sense of what the going rate is. This is an expense that pays back in dividends, so while you don't want to overextend yourself, you should see it as an investment in your future career development.

kernels (algorithms that pick up key words) and AI screening to see if your experience, your background, and your résumé match what they're looking for. If your keywords don't match theirs, your résumé will never get picked up."

Geez, that sounds brutal. But remember all the advice about your profile and your elevator pitch. It's all there; you just need to repackage it a little each time. Both employers—and bots—can smell BS. Don't even think about sending a résumé completely written by AI. And maybe, if you're lucky, an actual human will read it.

Now, the Interview

To prepare for an interview, professional development specialist Lorraine K. Lee recommends prepping three things:

1. What experience do you bring to the table?

2. What are the unique skills, character traits, or values that describe you?

3. What is your personal story?

Take some time to think about "your unique value," says marketing expert Sylvia Long-Tolbert. "This is what branding is intended to do. Embedded in that should be a clear statement—the North Star about how you live your values." Who you are—in or outside the office.

Overwhelmed? Write It Down

You know that simple idea of keeping a notepad by the bed in case you want to remember a thought, a dream, or a random moment of sleepy brilliance? Well, the same goes for your brand. Think of it as a cheat sheet either to help you during a Zoom interview or to merely jog your memory and motivate yourself on an off day.

And, hey, they do this in the movies all the time (or, if you want to go full cinema, you could do a monologue in the mirror). What is your mission statement? You could just scribble down a bunch of keywords that get you fired up and give you joy. (One of Laura's words would be *joy*, actually. Also, *clever*, *subversive*, and *helpful*. Kristina's? *Inspiration*, *innovation*, and *impact*.) And it's totally fine to put some ego into it—you've worked hard!

"You have to know and believe your worth, how you performed, and what you've contributed," says Long-Tolbert. She recommends having two statements: a longer professional mantra and a tighter one for your "billboard." "If it's a LinkedIn tagline, it's twenty-five words. If it's an intro or overview to your résumé, give yourself maybe fifty words."

Lee agrees: "When you have a really tight message, it helps people remember who you are and also helps them understand why you are interested in that particular role."

Do a Practice Interview First

OK, say you are going for your dream job. Don't bet everything, including your interview performance, on that horse. Mizrachy has some great advice: "If you're setting up a few interviews, and you're allowed flexibility, schedule your second-choice employer first. Don't go for your best job interview first.

"It's sort of like dating. Get out there, practice a little bit, see what it's like. When you've had a couple of practice rounds, then you're more ready to go after that dream job." Hey, maybe after a few go-rounds, you'll even identify your lucky interview shirt. It's all key research and practice to get you closer to your main goal.

Identify Your "Star Stories"

Look back to what you wrote on your résumé—you already have a template for this. Easy! Marianne Ruggiero, founder of Optima Careers, says, "When you write a résumé, you should be putting bullet points around accomplishments. People want to know how you create value. Prepare star stories [former workplace triumphs like revenue, press, or awards] to tell people about what you've accomplished."

How to Talk About Your Layoff in an Interview

Be honest (someone smarter than us once said it's the best policy—thanks, Benjamin Franklin!). "It's not something that you should be ashamed of," Gavin says. "If you're asked about it in an interview, you can answer the question very directly: 'The company decided to do a reduction in force, and I was unfortunately caught up in that wave. I was appreciative of the opportunity to build my skills and experience in that role, and I'm now looking forward to an opportunity to take those skills to this company.'"

Keep it high and tight. Nobody needs *War and Peace* on whatever the situation was that led you to this interview. "The more time you spend talking about it, the more it seems like there's *more* to it," Gavin says. In short, don't give your layoff so much power over you, and don't beg even more questions.

Stay Positive and Don't Badmouth

No matter what your feelings are about your former employer, resist the urge to vent. Trash-talking your old company—or former colleagues—will make you look not just unprofessional but obsessed with the past. Which is just weird. Instead, stick to neutral, forward-looking statements like "I'm grateful for the experience I gained in the role, but I'm excited for this next chapter." What do they call it? Public relations.

Be Prepared to Explain Your "Break" if They Ask

With so much change in the workplace, employers are generally more empathetic about time passing between jobs. LinkedIn career expert Catherine Fisher says, "That hiring manager probably also knows someone personally who has lost their job. With that stigma going away, it's totally fine to say, 'I am back in the job market. I took six months off, and I'm actively interviewing now.' And during this time off, let's say, 'I noticed that AI is now in every conversation. So, I took these courses to really understand how to use AI.'

"Being specific about what you did to continue learning during that break is absolutely applicable to the role that you are applying for."

Burned Out from Job Searching?

If you've gone weeks or months without getting a bite and are feeling so frustrated from filling out job applications and writing cover letters, you may be doing yourself more harm than good. Workplace mental health strategist Natasha Bowman says, "You're not doing yourself any justice if you are burned out before you even start your new job. Take breaks throughout your process, and let the résumé sit there. You've put in enough. Trust the universe for a while, regroup, and engage in things again that you enjoy.

"A lot of times that burnout doesn't come from 'Oh, I'm sitting and I'm having to redo résumé after résumé after résumé.' It comes from 'I don't feel like I'm doing something fulfilling and purposeful by tailoring my résumés all day.' Stop for a few days and do something fulfilling and purposeful."

Mizrachy recommends, "Take yourself off the job market for a short period of time. If you're not desperate for a salary, try to volunteer in the area that you're interested in. Use your network to say, 'Look, give me a three-month trial. I'll be free labor for you. I want to listen. I want to learn. I want to be busy. I want to have a sense of purpose. I want to have a sense of focus.'

"The bonus is you're actually plumping your résumé. So, you'll legit be able to add something new and interesting. You're testing out a different industry and opportunity—and you're giving yourself a mental, physical, and emotional reprieve."

Also, take some time to study. Mizrachy adds, "Take a certification in something, do an online program—maybe a short one—but use the time to your advantage so that you come out of that period better."

Be sure to manage your day so you're not drowning in repetition. Fisher says, "Give yourself specific goals. Like, 'OK, from eleven to one, I'm going to focus on my job search, and then I'm going to take a break.' Having that discipline in terms of timing and how you're approaching the job search is important."

Take Something That Isn't Your Dream Job if It Helps Get You Where You Want to Be

Remember, Mika Brzezinski did this by taking a newsreader demotion. Think of it as a refueling on the way to your destination. Ruggiero says, "Even if you take a job you don't really want to do but it gets you to the right company, then once you do a good job for a year or two, people will know you. Now they'll let you do something you've never done before." You'll also have more flexibility to move around the company because your employer trusts you. "I think people tend to put a lot of emphasis on the job and don't spend enough time evaluating the platform or the organization," Ruggiero adds.

She gives an example: "So, maybe I'm in social media marketing and I want to go to HR. Nobody's going to hire you to do HR. You've never done it before. So, you go to Nike and you do social media marketing. You do it really well, and you say, 'I've learned the company. I really like the people, but I'd rather serve the employees than the customers. Could I do some marketing for recruiters and help them find better candidates?'

"Then the company is more likely to give you a shot because you're an internal candidate. Maybe compromise the job, take the best you can do, but really focus on trying to get into the best organization so that you can upgrade once you get there."

It's called playing the long game.

Pick Up Freelance Work to Buy Yourself Time

You need to make some money? Take some freelance work you can do well without buying into too much emotionally. Ruggiero says, "The benefit of being fired and being available is that you can date without getting married. So, it's the opportunity to potentially freelance or consult, depending upon what level you're at. Pick up a project and say, 'I want to think through what I want to do, but I certainly would be happy to help out with a project.' You can use the buy-time strategy until you figure out what exactly—or if you know what you want to do but it's not available at that moment."

Important! When a Job Offer Is Not Right, Just Say No

Don't be the jerk in knee-jerk, grabbing the first possible gig that comes along because you're in a panic. If something isn't right, be gracious. Gavin says, "It's OK to say, 'Thank you so much. That opportunity is not quite the right fit for me, but I really appreciate you sending it along. Thank you again so much for thinking of me.' Just be grateful."

"Do not feel like you have to pursue every phone call," says Ruggiero. "You can just say, 'I decided I want to take a time-out and think through what I want to do going forward. Let me call you back when I'm ready.'"

16

Lindsay Colas

> Lindsay Colas is executive vice president, Talent + The Collective, at sports management firm Wasserman. She has been hired and fired by clients for over twenty years.

"Even when you've done everything right, there's always something to learn."

What Happened

I've never been fired from a job where I received a W-2, but I've definitely been fired by clients. I think most agents with a significant roster have been fired at some point. I've been doing this for twenty years now, representing women's basketball players. My first client was [WNBA Phoenix Mercury basketball player] Diana Taurasi, who retired in the spring after a twenty-season WNBA run; I've represented her since her second year, so over nineteen years. In my industry, you're bound to get fired by clients for various reasons—sometimes for reasons that have nothing to do with you.

One of the first times I remember having the feeling of failure wasn't even with a client—it was when I ran for ninth-grade class president and lost. I had been president in seventh and eighth grades, but I ran a lazy campaign in ninth grade. I mailed it in, thinking I had it in the bag. I wasn't prepared, and I got beaten by someone who'd taken their campaign very seriously. Someone who, perhaps, I had not taken seriously. That lesson about not being prepared, or when you assume an outcome, has stayed with me.

Fast-forward to my career, and I've had to part ways with clients under different circumstances. One of my first big moments wasn't exactly getting fired, but I had to fire a client. There came a moment when her behavior began to compromise my business, so I needed to consider whether I could continue representing her. That was a tough decision to make, but it taught me about setting boundaries.

Agenting is really difficult because it is a constant challenge to help clients understand the amount of background work you do that goes into their business. The only thing that matters to them is the results. There's no A for effort. It's not "show your work," and you get half credit from the math teacher. Ultimately, you are evaluated based on what you can or can't deliver.

What makes me good at what I do is that I'm extremely creative. Being a woman with so much experience in an industry like this, we come up with ideas that provide for a lot of firsts. A lot of pioneering work, which is hard and rewarding. We seek firsts, not to be the first and only forever, but to create space not to be the last. Approaching representation in sports as a woman is different from how men have historically approached representation. We approach it from an abundance mindset versus a scarcity mindset, where we don't see every opportunity as being zero-sum, like this or that, or him or her. Instead, if we can create an opportunity with one client, there will be a way to level up for others so that their success should mean opportunity for others.

I saw a statistic recently that said only 6 percent of Fortune 500 companies are spending money on women's sports, but it feels like there's all this momentum, and there's a tremendous amount of competition. Until three years ago, we were the only [sports] agency other than Octagon who had a dedicated women's practice—now all the agencies are there, the UTAs [United Talent Agency], the CAAs [Creative Artists Agency], the Klutches [Klutch Sports Group]. Nobody else had a women's practice. They literally said in their values that women didn't matter. I was beating my head against the wall for fifteen years before everyone else said, "Oh, wow, this is a really interesting business."

My client [WNBA Phoenix Mercury basketball player] Brittney Griner's detention in Russia in 2022 was an inflection point. We represent many of the best, the brightest, the most successful, and the leaders of many sports. All of them, for the most part, showed up for the fight to free Brittney. When I asked clients, "I need you to do CNN," or whatever, everybody showed up. It was a true collective effort, and it was very, very rewarding. It also was extremely taxing, and it was hard on my family, because it was actually life or death. You wake up in the morning, and you go to bed at night, and you can't find enough time in the day to have all the conversations you want to have. This went on for ten months.

During this time, our clients gave us a lot of grace, but it gave our competitors ammunition to say, "She couldn't possibly be thinking about you. She's thinking about [Brittney]." After Brittney came home, a client's parents called me, and I thought they were calling to congratulate me.

Instead, they fired me. They said all the usual things like, "You've done so much for women's sports, and we respect you," but then they said they were "going in a different direction." I had just helped negotiate an international life-or-death situation, and then this happened.

What Next

After that firing, I remember crying. It was such a gut punch. But, over time, I've learned to assess what went wrong in those situations, even when I know I did a great job. Sometimes there are factors beyond your control, and you need to accept that.

Being fired by a client doesn't just impact me personally—it affects my whole team. They work incredibly hard, and it's tough when all that effort feels unrecognized. It's not just an ego hit; it affects the morale of the people who have put their time and energy into these clients. But over the years, I've learned that this business is cyclical. Clients come and go, and sometimes they just need a change. It doesn't always mean we did something wrong.

There was one situation where I was fired by a client but then rehired by her a couple of years later. I had just had my second baby and was coming back from maternity leave. I hadn't been as plugged in with her as I should have been, and she left. It was painful. But when she came back, our relationship was stronger because of the honesty we were able to have with each other. We both grew from that experience.

What I Learned

Getting fired is never easy, but I've learned so much from those experiences. Even when you've done everything right, there's always something to learn. I've come to see that being fired gives you the opportunity to reflect on your own actions, evaluate where things might have gone wrong, and apply those lessons moving forward. It gives you the wherewithal to stand up and evaluate: What role did I play? Where did I fail? How could I be better?

It's important to take ownership of what happened and not just chalk it up to bad luck or external forces. There's real value in assessing what you could have done differently, even if the situation was out of your control. I've found that failure often teaches you more than success.

Redefine Yourself in the Workplace

Supe Up Your Professional Brand

When you've been barreling through your career, barely noticing the years fly by—well, that and your incremental 3 percent raises—when do you ever take a minute to think about how you've grown, what you represent, and what you really, really want? Well, getting fired gives you that chance. Hey, thanks, Fired!

As we said earlier, Laura and Kristina approached this special gift in different ways. Laura took real time to see what broader opportunities might present themselves, while knowing that the day-to-day grind of fashion media no longer held her interest. She was her own boss now: "LB" was her brand.

Kristina was more mercenary. She knew her previous position as editor in chief (again, such a weird title) was too small a container for her future ambitions. She started excitedly rethinking how she could package and present herself beyond conventional journalistic roles. Her skills in storytelling, branding, and cultural curation could travel way, way beyond traditional media.

So, if you're aiming to interview better and land a job faster, now is the time to drill down and redefine yourself. Is your résumé frozen in 2020? Did you unlink from LinkedIn? Well, this is the *perfect* time to reframe yourself in the workplace. Update that bio, edit your social media, reconnect with contacts, and learn some new skills (even if it's knowing how to filter your tired ass on Zoom). The irony is, once you focus on *who you are*, you'll notice more doors swing open.

What's Your Brand?

This is not your Instagram grid: it's the person you want to project in your industry. But don't let the idea of your personal "brand" intimidate you: "Reframe the idea of a personal brand. It's simply just your reputation," says professional development specialist Lorraine K. Lee. "Your personal brand should authentically represent who you are and what you stand for. It's about aligning your external image with your internal values and using that as a foundation to build meaningful professional relationships.

"Everyone has a personal brand," Lee continues. "What's going to differentiate you from someone else is whether you are actually being intentional about yours. I think a lot of people these days think of 'personal brand' and they're like, 'Ew, slimy,' or 'I'm marketing myself,' or 'I'm always talking about myself.' But the first thing to do is to shift your mindset. You can have either a great personal brand or a not-great one, but regardless, you have one."

While LinkedIn is a pivotal tool in building your brand (and what we'll spend most of this chapter focusing on), it's important to maintain a consistent presence across all the platforms you appear on. Employers will look up your "socials," so think before you post.

A good social media rule of thumb: not every feeling needs to be a billboard, especially sensitive geopolitical issues. Booz Allen Hamilton's Jill Mizrachy says, "If you have pretty extreme ideas about anything, I would be cautious with that. You can't, on the one hand, slam corporate America and then try to get a seven-figure job in corporate America. If you are applying for a job where inclusion and belonging are really important to that organization (and you have blatantly shared your more narrow opinions), there's a good chance the organization will see that and feel you are not a good fit."

Reboot Yourself on LinkedIn

A confession from both authors: we didn't really exist on LinkedIn before we were fired. We didn't think we needed it, and we didn't think it was cool. (Well, actually, Laura was there but paid so little attention that her profile for some reason listed her as an Italian accountant. Don't laugh. Actually . . . do.)

Kristina, on the other hand, used LinkedIn purely as a research tool during her ten years at *WSJ*. She'd log on occasionally to check someone's job title or see if they were still at a company—usually when she was hiring—but never gave her own profile more than a passing thought. It wasn't until after being laid off that she realized she needed to give it a real college try. With the help of a coach from the outplacement training package her company offered, she crafted her "About" section, updated her work experience, and started using the platform as more than just a glorified phone book.

Anyway, we were stupid. LinkedIn is fantastically useful. It's both your billboard and your newsletter, a super-engaged platform to communicate with your professional world—and humanize your professional story. This is the place where your brand can shine. Here are some key steps to make LinkedIn work for you.

Update Your Profile

Ideally, do this right away. Having an old profile sitting there isn't ideal, but it's not the end of the world. Executive recruiter Kristy Hurt says, "When I'm interviewing people, and their LinkedIn and résumé still shows 'present' at their employer and they really left fourteen months ago, it doesn't turn me off because I understand that no one knows how to navigate this. It's scary and it can take a really long time to find the next job, especially if at a more senior level."

That said, "If it's been more than a few months, I usually say, 'Let's just call it and say you're no longer there.'" Update that sucker! It will also be a nice turn of the mental page.

Tweak the "Months" on Your Résumé so Gaps Aren't Obvious

On your résumé, you *can* cook the books a little bit. Merge your jobs a little closer together. Hurt says, "Let's pretend someone gets fired in April of 2024 and starts a new job in February 2025. That's a ten-month gap. I would typically advise them to remove months on the résumé and just say, 'Former job, 2019 to 2024. Current job, 2025 to present.' Because then the gap months disappear, and no one needs to focus on it."

Update Your "About" Section

This is both your autobiography and greatest hits, where you can really tell your professional story. "You want to think of this as your elevator pitch," LinkedIn career expert Catherine Fisher says. "I always recommend including examples of the impact that you've had and why. Anyone can say, 'I'm great at sales,' but back that up with specific examples of the impact that you had on a business." That gets attention.

Most importantly, keep it tight. Who you are, what you do, and what you've done well—that's it.

Update Your "Skills" Section

Kill 'em with them skills! Communication, leadership, and management (if they are suited to you) are particularly compelling. "If you have at least one skill, you're going to receive up to two times more profile views and connection requests and four times as many messages," Fisher explains. And this section doesn't just synopsize what you can do; it might give you options outside your current industry that you may never have considered.

Fisher gives an example of Covid's impact on employment. "While some industries were shedding jobs, other industries had a hard time hiring—for example, health care. What they found is that instead of looking at the same pool of people [over and over], it was more about the *skills* that they were looking for. Suddenly, it was less about the industry where you were previously employed and more about the skills you have. Say you're a terrific communicator in the tech industry. You can take those skills and apply them to the entertainment industry. It's the same skill."

Join Conversations and Comment on Posts

Call it professional proof of life. Fisher says, "It doesn't mean you have to have a newsletter or write a ten-paragraph post, but you want to be participating and talking. Having conversations keeps you active, and those will show up when the recruiter is looking for you. It also gives you a really good perspective in terms of what's happening in the industry. It could just be adding a comment to someone's post. It's a simple way to network."

Commenting is also "a great way to get on the radar of someone," adds Lee. "If you can engage with someone's content, that can be a really nice differentiator. When I see people show up in my comments regularly and then they reach out with a message, I'm more likely to respond to them because I'm familiar with their face. They're engaging with my stuff and don't feel as much like a stranger to me."

Post on Your Newsfeed

Your profile is important, but posting content to the newsfeed is your real showcase. Lee says, "I view the profile as the foundation, but it is really the content creation that can elevate you to the next level. That's where you share more about who you are and how you think about the topics that you're passionate about, that you have expertise in." Spoke at a conference? Post a clip. Have a perspective on news in your industry? Share that, too.

Don't Send a Connection Request Without a Personalized Message

If you want to connect with someone who can further your career, Lee says, "In the note section, you have three hundred characters. It's not a ton of space, but it's enough for you to introduce yourself, share who you are and why you are reaching out." Customize it, keep it tight, and "use your elevator pitch to explain why they might want to accept your request. That will really increase the chances of your request getting accepted."

And if you're not accepted right away, don't take it personally. Sometimes people are just busy. When they do finally check out their page, they'll often find dozens of great people waiting to connect with them.

Just keep your eyes on the prize and tabs on what the person is up to. "Going in with just a connection request and a message might not get you accepted because this person is just busy and they don't know who you are," Lee says. But someone else will have a minute to connect, and you can build from there.

Ask for Recommendations from Former Colleagues

"LinkedIn is essentially Yelp for professionals," says Lee. You may have two profiles that look very similar—similar experience, similar skills—but you really need that social proof to stand out. To have recommendations or testimonials from managers, peers . . . a speaker from a conference, these are all fair game."

A recruiter is drowning in profiles and trying to make quick decisions, so stack the deck. Be obvious. Show off a little bit, it's fine. "Even if it's a few recommendations and people writing glowing things about you, that's a huge advantage and differentiator."

Mark Yourself as "Open to Work"

Again, it's OK to be obvious. You want a job, tell people! The "open to work" tag is in your photo frame, so switch it on. Fisher says, "On average, 40 percent of people are more likely to receive InMails from recruiters if they have that on." And 20 percent are more likely to receive messages from LinkedIn notes.

But if you are a little shy about being so . . . open, "What's cool about 'open to work' is that you can either do it publicly with your network or do it privately and just have that signal to recruiters," Fisher adds. "It's really up to you in terms of how much you want to share."

Use "Job Preferences"

Following the vast change in the working landscape post-Covid, LinkedIn added "Job Seeking Preferences." Here you can say if you want remote or hybrid work and list the types of companies and roles you are interested in. "What that will do is allow LinkedIn to serve up roles that you may not have considered," Fisher explains. Think of it as more options on the career buffet: "It is really about having an open mind."

Set Up Job Alerts and Apply as Soon as You Can

Alert, alert! We have alerts for everything on our phones (hello news, hello Instagram, hello . . . step-tracking), so set up the job ones, stat. According to LinkedIn, "People who apply within the first ten minutes are four times more likely to hear back about a position."

Make Sure Recruiters See Your Profile

If there's a job you really want and are applying for, emulate it with your profile. "Look at that job description, see how they're prioritizing the skills, and make sure that you're doing the same in your profile," Fisher says. Basically: add those exact same skills to your profile—if you have them! This is not the time to BS, but it's a handy shorthand for recruiters to see the synergy between the role and, well, you.

Tips on Your Profile Photo

There is nothing weirder than seeing a picture of someone you know professionally, but it's, er, a decade old. It automatically looks unreliable. "You want to make sure that it's updated and that people are seeing the current you," Fisher advises. "Your headshot is really defined by how you live your professional life.

"For me, I am a little bit more formal, so that's going to be my profile photo. Whereas someone who is in a creative role may choose to be more creative in terms of their profile photo. And make sure it's shoulders and up. The photo isn't that big, so you want to be able to see the person. It's like dressing for the job you want to have."

Pay attention to the quality and lighting of your photo to ensure it portrays you in the best light possible. This photo is often your first impression in the digital professional world, so make it count. Choose an expression that feels like you, but also matches the tone of your industry—whether it's approachable, serious, or creative. To wit: Laura is full body on a set of stairs, because she really liked the legs on her pantsuit, while Kristina's is on point and perfectly cropped in black and white.

Use LinkedIn's AI Tools

There are quite a few nifty tools and shortcuts that can help you out if you're just staring vacantly at a blinking cursor.

- Conversational Job Search. You can search for jobs in the same way you'd ask a question, using plain language to find a role that's the best fit for you.

- Résumé Review. Get tailored recommendations on your résumé to save time and showcase your most relevant skills.

- Cover Letter Assistance. The AI tool can help you draft a compelling cover letter for a given role from scratch. Of course, you should absolutely personalize your letter, but it gets you going. Your letter should automatically include relevant information and package up your experience. By covering the baseline, you are free to add voice and character. And remember, your human skills are what gets you a job in the end, not artificial intelligence.

The beauty of LinkedIn is that it's a one-stop shop, and whether you find your next job there or not, it's a sanctioned professional destination where anyone, from anywhere in the world, can easily find you (like Facebook, but without your uncle Jerry). Talk about workplace efficiency!

Carol Burnett

Carol Burnett is the first lady of American comedy. She starred in the groundbreaking *Carol Burnett Show* from 1967 to 1978. At ninety-two, she is currently featuring on *Palm Royale*. She was fired from her usherette job at Warner Brothers Theatre in 1951.

> "The biggest lesson I learned from losing my job was that it doesn't end there. There's always some place to go; there's always more to happen."

What Happened

In 1951, I was eighteen years old, and on a summer break from college at UCLA. I got a job as an usherette at the Warner Brothers Theatre [now the Hollywood Pacific Theatre] on Hollywood Boulevard. I was paid sixty-five cents an hour. We had to wear these very strange, funny uniforms: a velvet top with epaulettes at the shoulders and balloon harem pants. And like a fez hat.

The manager, Mr. Batton, was certifiable. He was really nuts. He would give us a signal as to where he wanted us to report. He would hold up two fingers if he wanted you to be in front of the door at aisle two, three fingers for aisle three. He would make a C with his fingers, and that meant go behind the candy counter. And we would have to salute and march to our positions. Yes, salute.

Now remember, this was back in the covered wagon days when movies would run constantly, on a loop. So, people would come in and want to be seated right in the movie when it was halfway through! Then they would wait and see it start all over again, get to the point where they came in, and then leave.

I was a true movie nut, and I felt nobody should come in the middle of a movie; they should see it from beginning to end. This one night, Mr. Batton had me in front of the aisle two door. We were showing a wonderful Alfred Hitchcock movie called *Strangers on a Train*. So, this couple came in and wanted to be seated in the last five minutes of *Strangers on a Train*, which would ruin the entire movie for them. I said, "No, please don't sit down now. It will ruin it for you. It will start again in ten minutes." Well, they insisted they wanted to sit down. But I was adamant: "This is Hitchcock!"

Now, Mr. Batton hears this going on, and he comes up and says, "What's going on here?" And this woman complains, "She won't let us sit down." And I said, "Mr. Batton, it's *Hitchcock*. It'll be over in three minutes." He looked at me, and he said, "Burnett!" And I said, "Yes?" and he ran his index finger across his neck like he was cutting my head off. He said, "You're fired." And he ripped off my epaulettes, one by one, and pointed me to the downstairs changing room. (My fez was still on, by the way.) I was fired at sixty-five cents an hour.

I was distressed because I was living with my grandmother—she raised me—and we lived a block away in one room with a pull-down Murphy bed. I slept on the couch. I thought, "Oh my God." We barely made our rent of thirty dollars a month. For me, sixty-five cents an hour, well, that was money! I felt so terrible telling her that I got fired. She said, "Well, why didn't you let them sit down?" She was a little angry: "You shouldn't have done that." But then, as luck would have it, an opening came up across the street with another theater, the Iris. They hired me to be in the box office, and I got seventy-five cents an hour! I got a dime raise.

I was at the Iris Theatre for the rest of the summer, and then I went back to UCLA in the fall.

What Next

I was still living with my grandmother when I was at UCLA. I would take the streetcar and the bus to school. Take a guess what the tuition was back in 1952? Forty-three dollars. I wanted to go to UCLA after I graduated from Hollywood High, but my grandmother said we couldn't afford that tuition.

But I said, "Nanny, I know I'm going to get to go." I don't know how, but I saw myself on campus. I visualized myself on campus. It's gonna happen, it's gonna happen.

But here's another strange story. The room we lived in faced the manager's desk and mailboxes in the lobby. Every morning I would look out to see if we had a letter or something. One morning there was a letter. The envelope had my name, a typewritten address on it, and a three-cent stamp. I opened it up, and there was a fifty-dollar bill.

To this day, I don't know where that came from. My grandmother didn't have the money. The whole neighborhood was poor. Nobody had that kind of money. If any of my relatives had it, they would have said, "Look what I'm doing for you, dear." That fifty-dollar bill was my ticket to UCLA.

When I got to UCLA, I wanted to major in journalism, but it wasn't offered as a major. I looked in the catalog and found "Theater Arts/English," where I could take a playwriting course, because I wanted to write. But if you were majoring in theater arts, as a freshman you had to take an acting course—costumes, scenery, and all of this stuff. So, here I am, a freshman, taking this acting course, and I had never performed in my life.

The first time I was onstage was in the classroom. There were about fourteen of us in the class. I came in late, so the teacher gave me a monologue to do. I was terrible. She gave me a D-plus. She said, "The only reason I'm not failing you is because you memorized it."

But later we did some other scenes. Remember, I was in love with the movies when I was a kid, and I loved Betty Grable, all those movie stars. I had a scene to do, an offbeat musical thing, and I pretended to be Betty Grable. And I got an A. Some of the kids in the class said, "You were really good. Would you like to try out for the homecoming show or the varsity show?" Some seniors said, "You were really funny. Would you like to have lunch with us?" (That was like getting an Oscar.) All of a sudden, I became a performer, and it was all an accident.

When I realized that's what I wanted to do, I didn't want to tell my grandmother or my mother, because they would say, "What are you thinking? Are you crazy?" It took a while before I told them. The fact there wasn't a major in journalism changed my whole life.

After I graduated, I moved to New York. I had one phone number, and it was from a girl from UCLA who had gone to New York. I called her, and she said, "Where are you?" I was staying at a hotel, which was a lot of money—nine dollars a day, you know? She said, "Get out of there."

She was living at a place called The Rehearsal Club, a brownstone on West 53rd Street that housed young women who wanted to be in the theater. It was very, very strict, on the up and up. She introduced me to what they called the house mother, who said, "Well, we have one cot we can give you, and it's eighteen dollars a week, room and board. (It was sponsored by a lot of rich ladies in New York, which is why the rent was so low.)

That was the first time I'd ever slept on something other than a couch. I slept on couches until I was twenty-one. My first bed was that cot at The Rehearsal Club.

When it came to ability, I always knew I had it. When I got the chance to go to New York, I grabbed it because, I said, "It's going to happen." Some of my friends at UCLA gave me a bon voyage party. They said, "What are you going to do when you get to New York?" I said, "Well, someday I'm going to be in a Broadway show directed by George Abbott." Mr. Abbott was the premier director of musical comedies and Broadway at that time—and that's what eventually happened.

Before that, I worked. I did summer stock. I finally got to an agent, and he said, "Let me know when you're in something." And I said, "I can't get *in* something unless I have an agent." He said, "Go put on your own show." So, I went back to The Rehearsal Club, called the meeting of all the girls, and said, "We're going to put on a show." I got that idea from seeing all the Mickey Rooney and Judy Garland movies as a kid. They put on song-and-dance shows all the time.

So, we did. Agents and producers came, and I got an agent. Then, this one afternoon, the phone rang, and it was a couple who were producing a little show called *Once Upon a Mattress*. And they said, "Would you come down and audition for George Abbott?" I went down, I auditioned, and by the time I got home, the phone was ringing. I got the lead in *Once Upon a Mattress*, directed by George Abbott, in 1959. It was like when I saw myself on campus and got to go to UCLA. I honestly feel like I have a little angel on my shoulder.

But I remember I was up for a role before I got the play, and it was narrowed down to me and another girl. I really thought I had it. But she got it. You know what saved me? I said to myself, "You know what? It's not my turn. My turn will come."

Oh, here's a nice story. Years later, in 1975, when I got my star on the Hollywood Walk of Fame, they asked me where I wanted it. I said, "Put it right in front of the old Warner Brothers Theatre, on Hollywood Boulevard and Wilcox Avenue."

Then, to top it off, when they were renovating the theater three or four years ago, my husband asked what they were going to do with the aisle two door. They said, "Well, we're just going to get rid of it." He said, "Can we have it?" So, now the door I was fired in front of leads into our office at home.

What I Learned

My grandmother and I would save our pennies. And in the '40s, we would go to the movies a lot. That was my escape. Everything was positive in those days—the good guys got it; the bad guys didn't. There was no cynicism. So, somehow it imprinted itself on me. I never doubted myself. It wasn't like I was conceited or anything; it was just like, OK, my turn will come.

We used to go to the Grauman's Chinese Theater courtyard, where they had all the handprints and things. I remember putting my little handprints on Betty Grable's handprints. I was ten or eleven years old. Last year I was honored with a handprint and footprint ceremony there. I said, "Eighty years ago, when I put my handprints on Betty Grable's, little did I dream that I would be doing this today." And here I am, ninety-one years old. Maybe some kid will put their handprints on mine someday.

The biggest lesson I learned from losing my job was that it doesn't end there. There's always someplace to go; there's always more to happen. And that's what happened with the Iris Theatre.

My advice for women who've been fired? It's not over. There are other mountains to climb, other things to do, to win. Hang in there, and don't think that it's over. But you know, I was lucky. I had the attitude that I grew up with by watching the old movies. I credit that for my optimism. Mickey and Judy, oh boy, they never took no for an answer. If you have the fire in the belly, keep at it.

And sometimes, like my kid sister used to say—and it's a cliché—when one door closes, another one opens. Especially when it's the door from aisle two.

19

Screw It, Take a Break

A Little Rest Goes a Long Way

If you're able to, or *when* you're able to, get the hell outta Dodge. Maybe it's right after you've been canned, or maybe it's after you've hung around a bit, taken some meetings, and are just . . . tired. Perhaps you're feeling beaten down from all the hustling and frustrated that it hasn't landed you that dream job yet. There is no downside to taking a break in order to help get your mojo back so you can clear your head and reengage with the business at hand.

This could mean anything from leaving for an extended trip to going home to see your family to reboot your emotional system. At the very least, start taking long walks regularly and maybe listen to an audiobook for a little extra mental escape. Whatever works. The world from which you are briefly (and blessedly, trust us) uprooted is not going anywhere. Remember that people are consumed with themselves (remember Sallie Krawcheck's quote: "Nobody else cares") and are like goldfish, as in they have zero memories: if you peace out for a while, they'll be thrilled to see you when you're back. You'll be a novelty!

After they got married, Laura and her husband, Brandon, went on a honeymoon for so long, it became an extended vacation. Laura had worked her ass off for twenty-eight damn years, so she thought, "Eff it," and kicked the can a little—well, a lot—farther down the road. Of course, she had a little income and savings cushion, but either way, it's an interesting exercise, knowing that your brain and soul need a big ol' break—and deciding to give that to yourself. Despite what the "having it all" cliché tries to force on women, knowing your limitations, and precisely how broad your bandwidth is at any given time, is a blessing.

Kristina called the period after leaving *WSJ* and before starting at Sotheby's her "In Between Time." Coincidentally, her last day at *WSJ* was also her kids' last day of school, ushering in her "at home era." She shifted from the relentless pace of work to the rhythm of home life—cooking Alison Roman recipes (pretty well, actually), laboring over laundry, and chauffeuring her children wherever they needed to go. It was a deliberate busyness, pulling her away from the urge to sit at her computer, waiting for an email to change everything. She needed the summer off—things would pick back up in September.

That didn't mean she wasn't laying the groundwork, but why not enjoy the slower pace? She went to the beach alone in the middle of the week, devoured that stack of books on the nightstand, and sipped a glass of wine at 4 p.m. without an ounce of guilt. After all, it helped manage the inbox.

Decompress, Even for Just a Day

Obviously, most of the working population is not in the fortunate economic position where they can take an extended break. "But you can take a break for that first day," says career coach Phoebe Gavin. "You don't need to get on the job search immediately as soon as you find out."

Take that break because your brain (and maybe even your wee heart) has been broken. "Take a beat for at least that first day because you are going to make your worst decisions at that moment. Your emotions are going to be at the absolute highest. So, unless you have been very deeply therapized [or are a human Buddha], you probably don't have the coping mechanisms necessary to make good decisions that day. Experiencing maximum-level anxiety, insecurity, anger, frustration, resentment—all of the most difficult emotions—they make us make our worst decisions."

Your mind is literally spinning, so sit the hell down. "Take some time to process, and don't react immediately because it can be very scary, very upsetting," executive recruiter Kristy Hurt adds. "Just take a moment." And remember, *nobody cares*, and nobody is standing there with a stopwatch. So, take a minute.

Treat Yourself (Within Reason)

Taking time to reset means different things to different people, finances aside. *The New York Times* Your Money columnist Ron Lieber advises, "The question you have to ask yourself is: 'What is going to put me in the best position to take whatever mental reset I need to march forward with the maximum energy and confidence?' For some people, that might be, 'I'm going to get my 10K running time below forty-five minutes.' And for some people, that's going to be like, 'I'm going to fucking go to Maui. That's how I'm going to do the reset.'"

So, you do you! But remember, he adds, "The question of whether anything like that is borderline irresponsible or completely unwise depends on the amount of money that's sitting around after the severance, and who's depending on you. But I mean, I certainly wouldn't rule it out."

We've always liked Ron.

Want to Take a Grand Trip? Do It! (Sensibly)

Firstly and most obviously, check your finances. What can you afford without spending your entire "break" in a flop sweat? Ellevest's senior financial planner Sofia Figueroa says, "You don't want it to be a revenge spend situation where you're like, 'I'm going to go on an all-out vacation to totally decompress because I deserve it.'

"I think if it's possible, you can totally do it, but that's where taking advantage of things like credit card points, rewards, hotel points, or airline miles can be really helpful. That will reduce the cost of the trip."

Also, be honest about your job possibilities before you board that plane, train, or automobile. "See what your prospects are and how much runway you have. If you've got six months of expenses and income in the bank, you're probably not going to feel as stressed out about spending a chunk of that on something that's not an absolute necessity. If you're more on the side of two to three months and you're in a specialized field—or you're really only willing to accept a certain compensation package—you may not want to spend right now."

Then find an alternative. "That could even be like, 'I'm going to do a little staycation—one night in a nice hotel in my town where it's going to cost me a couple hundred dollars rather than a full-blown week away.'" Again, remember a break isn't supposed to cause you more stress, so look at what you need, and spend what you can manage.

Either Way, Don't Let Timeline Pressure Cloud Your Judgment

Again, yes, you have rent and bills, but try to subdue that ticking clock. Andy Hamilton, CEO of health-care startup When, who previously worked at Expedia, says, "You need time to evaluate your options. I was closing down our division [at Expedia], so I had three months to know this was coming. I was mentally preparing myself for what I would do next. Before Covid, I had told myself I'm never doing another startup again. And then during those three months of winding down . . . you're not working as hard, things are shutting down, and you're mentally starting to take a break. For me it was reevaluating: 'Did I want to do this startup or did I want to go work for another company like Expedia?'

"I think it is important to give yourself time to recover from the prior job. You're not going to make your best decision if you either quit on your own or you get laid off or terminated and you're making a decision that next day. You need to think about things. Just like in any relationship, you've got to let the dust settle before you jump right back in."

So, if that is helped by lying down in your bed, your backyard, or at a luxury hotel, do it.

Angela Missoni & Margherita Maccapani Missoni

Angela Missoni left her role as Missoni's creative director of ready-to-wear in 2021, and Margherita Maccapani Missoni left her role as creative director of M Missoni in 2022.

> "Sometimes we don't have the guts to leave something that doesn't belong to us anymore, and life does us a favor in taking it away."

What Happened

ANGELA: My parents, Ottavio and Rosita Missoni, started our family-owned company in Italy in 1953. In 2018, the Italian investment fund Fondo Strategico Italiano (FSI) took a 41.2 percent stake in the company. When FSI came in, they decided they wanted to once again hire Margherita—who had previously worked at the company and was now doing her own thing—to be the creative director of M Missoni [Missoni's more accessibly priced line]. Margherita was a natural to follow me as creative director at Missoni, so, of course, I agreed.

From the first day onward, the investors kept asking me, "How long do you want to stay in your position? What do you think about your future?" I said, "I'm willing to stay while I'm needed. I don't need to do this job for my whole life; I just felt the company needs me. So, I'll be there to support the company."

Then, in 2020, during Covid, the company started having financial problems. That was the moment that we decided, together with FSI, to hire a CEO. He was good at handling money, so it seemed like the right choice for the moment. And we were still a small company, so it's not always easy to hire someone for that position.

The CEO came in and started pushing for Margherita to become creative director of the entire company [Angela Missoni had been creative director since 1997].

MARGHERITA: Luckily, my mother and I talked. I told my mom's boyfriend, Bruno, that I was really uncomfortable with the situation.

ANGELA: Then I had a meeting with FSI, and they said, "What do you think about the future? Would you let go, and have Margherita come in?" As I said from the beginning, I said, "I'm ready to leave if Margherita takes my position, no problem. I can stay on as president, but Margherita can be the creative director of Missoni and do everything that comes with it."

So, the process started. But two months later they asked everybody in the younger generation of the family [Margherita and her three cousins] to do a psychological assessment for human resources.

MARGHERITA: I didn't mind doing it because I had no reason to doubt them. I thought it was fair for everyone to do it, to understand their qualities and their flaws. And I was ready to work on my flaws.

The test showed that I was kind of a leader figure. My flaws were that I always tried to win in situations—I was not good at compromise. So, they told me that I had to improve that. And I'm like, yeah, I'm aware of that, and I will. But I had these definitive leader qualities, so I thought it was good.

ANGELA: At the same time, the CEO decided to close the M line and focus on Missoni. The process was to create one brand, Missoni, and for Margherita to be creative director.

MARGHERITA: And, you know, I was never keen on doing M Missoni. When they proposed it to me, I was working for myself. I wasn't working with my family. I started to become an "It girl," got a contract with Estée Lauder, and became a spokesperson. I had been traveling the world for many years. Then later I started working with my mother on design for the main line and doing beachwear, shoes, and handbags.

Then I left, and I became a mother. I also had a lot of great licensing deals happening, including my own children's-wear line; a Pottery Barn Kids collaboration; two seasons with Splendid. I was making really good money.

I didn't have to deal with production. I didn't have to deal with sales. I wasn't building anything—none of these were long-term projects—but I was not going back to the family company.

But FSI came to me and said, "This is part of the strategy. Part of Missoni's value is being a family company." They had to identify someone in the family who would be able to continue the business, right? So, they basically told me, "This is a make-or-break kind of deal. You're coming back and you're going to do M Missoni."

And I was like, that's a diffusion line; it's a copy of Missoni. It's not something that was appealing to me. But then I had an idea: let's boldly make this like the leftovers of Missoni—the elements that didn't fit in, didn't make it famous, that were left aside. So, I started working with upcycling, all the yarns, the fabrics, the archives, and the old prints and the cheesy 1980s advertisements for the perfume. All of which led to me saying, "OK, I'm going to do it," and I went back to the family business.

ANGELA: Remember, the idea was for Margherita to eventually run Missoni. But at the end of 2021, after the psychological assessment, the CEO decided Margherita was not going to be that person.

So, I was out. And she was out. Both of us were out. Officially,

Margherita declared in January 2022 that she was leaving, like it was her own choice.

MARGHERITA: They asked me to do that.

ANGELA: It's always "our choice," right?

MARGHERITA: I was not fazed that they would close M, because I always thought that M would eventually fold into Missoni, anyway. At the last meeting I had (my mom was there, too), I knew I was already out. I am very emotional, and I didn't want to show the CEO that, so I took a Xanax.

He proposed an ambassador deal, which was just a joke. And then he said, "The only value you have for this company is your last name. The sooner you learn that, the better off you'll be."

ANGELA: I don't even really remember it. It was so emotional.

MARGHERITA: I went back home, and my husband would always tell me that because of me and my job, we were stuck here in Varese, Italy. We could leave for six months on a sailing boat with the kids, and they couldn't take up these wonderful opportunities because of me and my ambition. And so, I went back home and said, "We can leave!" But the following summer, we broke up, and we got divorced later that year.

Eventually, the Missoni situation became public. Everybody felt sorry for us. They didn't know the details, but they thought the big finance guy came in and broke it.

What Next

ANGELA: The very next day after the news came out about Margherita leaving, Max Mara called her to do a collaboration for Max & Co., the first time in their history that the Max Mara group did a collaboration with another name. Somebody appreciated her talent.

MARGHERITA: It was a little sign. Signs are good when you start seeing them. Then you start trusting the process.

I had a hard time letting go because I never felt free to choose for my life. For almost forty years, I always felt like my path was set and written for me. I didn't enjoy that feeling. Although I did other things, I always knew that it was eventually heading in that direction at Missoni.

The following summer I got a call from a friend of my sister Teresa, a screenwriter, who was directing her first movie. She was like, "I don't know how to ask you this, but I'd love for you to play a role in this movie. You can think about it."

I had wanted to act when I was younger. I studied acting when I lived in New York. My passion was fashion, but I had to distance myself from it to understand myself.

So, when this opportunity presented itself, right away I was like, "I'm going to do it." I have nothing to lose. There are no expectations from people. I don't have a job.

After being fired, once I started feeling like myself again and could just be myself, change happened. I got this movie offer, which I took, and then I ended up going to the Venice Film Festival as an actress.

I am really grateful: I would never have dared to let go of my job. I would have never dared to let go of my marriage. And now, I can't believe my luck. I really feel blessed.

ANGELA: I was kind of serene. I was sorry for Margherita. And sorry for Missoni, because I still think it can be a very significant brand. It has a history and a story. I always thought that Missoni is like a rough diamond that could explode on the right path.

And I knew what I had done for Missoni, for almost thirty years. I had nothing to prove anymore. I know that I've done good work for the company. It was when I first started there that the moment totally changed in fashion, when fashion became luxury. Big groups, lots of muscle, and people became focused on luxury. So, to keep this small brand relevant, to keep the name shining in that world, I think, honestly, I made a miracle happen.

I'm sure that a name like Missoni will stay. If it's well managed, it can be a big opportunity.

What We Learned

ANGELA: Through all of it, I kept the family together. That was my big job. And to keep my mother safe [from all the corporate pressure involved in the company she founded; Rosita died in 2025]. My advice would be to concentrate on the family. I don't know what to say about how to handle it as a woman—but the thing is, by taking the women from Missoni, they took out the heart of the company.

When I became creative director of Missoni, I always thought I was going to do it for ten years, then, I believe, for fifteen years, and I'm grateful to be a daughter of such special parents. My mother was a natural builder. She put one brick on top of the other. But my father was always a free-spirited man with no material attachment to anything. Totally free. So, these thoughts were always in the back of my mind—that I could change my life from one day to another, to something else.

So, that's what helped me. When this whole situation happened, I was aware that things can change, and I was ready anyway. I have a lot of different passions, which definitely helps.

MARGHERITA: I learned to let go. I just had to trust the process and know that everything happens for a reason. Looking back, I lived too much in my head, and I should listen more to my body. But I'm really good at recognizing the past and where my choices took me. Each one took me somewhere.

ANGELA: Having children helped me be more understanding of the rest of the world, to be more open to other points of view. I've always been maternal in my job—attached to people, always trying to build harmony.

I know I was privileged because it was my parents' company. I was lucky my mom let me do this job. And she gave me *her* job, right? Then she let me go and do it.

MARGHERITA: Was my value tied to my job? I don't think so. Rather than worrying about what other people thought, I started thinking about how my kids saw all of this and saw me. I wanted them to see me as strong throughout this time, to see me thriving, you know? But obviously it takes some time. They also need to see that you can come out of it. And my value, more than my job, has always been tied a lot more to my role as a mother.

My new brand, Maccapani (my other last name) is doing really well. I had an idea, which was making a collection out of jersey, which has the comfort of knitwear but keeps its shape. Very feminine, but functional. We launched a year ago, and I have a good group of investors.

I went out and asked for money, which was the hardest thing for me. I grew up in a family of working women, the capital of the family, but I still had that thing: culturally, girls are not brought up to talk about money. I really got out of my comfort zone, and I was really proud. Maccapani is a small company, but yeah, it's a happy ending.

ANGELA: Through all my years at Missoni, it wasn't always shiny. I had many moments where I felt low, like somebody was trying to take me down. But I was always like those plastic things that you punch, and they bounce back up. I was like, that's me. In the end, I am a fighter.

All my life, I've always been good at analyzing what happens and being very clear about why and what. I'm happy that Margherita has basically grown up the same way.

But something that I've learned recently—because I've been very lucky through the years—is that somebody could play tricks with me. I can only blame myself for being too open. I always had a lot of trust in people: when they say they're doing something, I believe them. But maybe sometimes, you need to be a bit more...

MARGHERITA: ... on guard. The most important thing I've learned about getting fired is that sometimes we don't have the guts to leave something that doesn't belong to us anymore, and life does us a favor in taking it away. New things won't flow in and find us until we create space for them. It's a necessary step to reach the next stage. Life is built of different phases, and change is intrinsic. It isn't easy, but life knows best. We don't.

21

Firing Yourself

When It's Time to Walk Away and Plan Your Next Move

It's happened. You've been at your job a while and you've got the ick. There are endless closed-door meetings and random "consultants" wandering around, but there's no corporate communication. A quick read of the room will make it clear that the vibes are off.

If you're not confident in your position, you don't know where you stand day to day or, worse, if you're even valued—well, get out of there, sister! Leave them before they leave you! Oh, and forget that "quiet quitting" nonsense; why would you want to passively prolong a situation that is chipping away at you every day?

In 2004, Laura worked at *Details* magazine for nine months, which felt like dog years. Right after she accepted the job, she was approached about a position at *Harper's Bazaar*. *Details* rapidly became a passive-aggressive, destabilizing mire. Laura had her *fugouttahere* epiphany when all her fellow senior editors were asked out to lunch with the editor in chief, but not her. Luckily, *Harper's Bazaar* called again. She started there in 2005, and stayed until 2016.

Kristina never fired herself but fantasized about it more than once. She loved her job at *Harper's Bazaar*—it was a career-defining chapter where she learned, grew, and thrived. But after twelve years, she was itchy. She was ready for something else, something new—where she'd be the one calling the shots. Energy-wise, she was putting herself out there—manifesting the next chapter by taking meetings and flicking her hair around the industry—which led to *WSJ. Magazine*, and subsequently, her current perch at *Sotheby's Magazine*.

But . . . back to you. Take inventory every six months about how you are feeling about your job and yourself in that job. Are you still learning? Do you feel challenged? Are you engaged by the work, the people? If you have more nos than yeses to these questions, you may want to think about making a move. You have agency—use it. But as tempting as it might be to do the full *Jerry Maguire* (Gen Z: YouTube it) or be like that guy on the internet who gave his boss a letter and played himself out with a full band, it's best to hatch a plan in advance.

Start looking at the job market, surf around on LinkedIn, take meetings, research adjacent jobs and industries if that's something you're interested in, and sail out the door with your power intact and options that you've spent careful time preparing.

How to Know When to Fire Yourself

Your Health Is Suffering

Not only can staying in the wrong job too long negatively affect you (irritable, cranky, distraught, depressed, anxious, obsessive—take your pick), but it can also set you up for disaster in your next role: "A lot of us suffer PTSD from toxic work environments," says workplace mental health strategist Natasha Bowman. "So, when we go to that new environment, we carry that with us. And that means we are analyzing every word, every behavior, every movement at this new job because we haven't fully digested and healed from the experience with our previous employer."

Remember, as we discussed at the beginning of this book, your job is not your identity. It is not your value. And your job never *owned* you. So, the faster you separate yourself from it, the better. "The only thing you were doing was lending your credibility, your value, and your talents to the organization. And the key word there is *lend*—not give, not own, you're lending." Bowman continues with an analogy: "You're like a book being returned to the library. Now someone who is more deserving of it can check the book out."

So, to bastardize Ice Cube, check out before you're wrecked.

You Can't Reach Your Long-Term Goals

If you feel like you're in *Groundhog Day*—but there's no Bill Murray—fire up your curiosity and start looking beyond the cubicle . . . sorry, horizon. You haven't been fulfilled by a project for months, you haven't gotten a raise, there is no promotion coming. "I think there comes a time in every job where you feel like your ability to learn more is at a plateau," says professional development specialist Lorraine K. Lee.

"The first time I quit was because I learned from that job that I wanted to do more writing. I have a journalism background, and it was a marketing job. The second time, I was at a very small startup. To be part of a larger team where I could learn from other people was important to me, so I quit the startup."

So, if you feel like a different structure will benefit you more, definitely investigate and put some feelers out. And if you want to manage people but aren't given opportunities to eventually do that, that's another reason to get moving. Lee worked at LinkedIn and enjoyed it, but the way it was structured made a management role unfeasible. "So, I had to decide, did it make sense to leave? I wasn't super actively looking, but I found the right opportunity. It was a new challenge that excited me. I could take everything I learned at LinkedIn and apply it to a more medium-sized startup."

Learning, curiosity, growth, all the therapy words: listen to them and prioritize them.

You've Lost Your Mojo

Are you still scuttling on that hamster wheel, with your days all starting to bleed into one another? Lee says, "When you feel like your days are all the same and you're not really getting what you want out of it, that's probably a good indicator that it's time to start thinking about it."

Great job performance comes from stimulation and commitment, so if neither of those are happening—well, you won't be happening either. If you're not learning anything new, not being challenged, and you're not producing at the level you used to, take a look in the mirror and recognize that. And think about taking a risk! What's the worst thing that can happen: you go back to a job just like your former one somewhere else. But with risk, as they say, comes reward.

Even more importantly, if you've forgotten about the things in your non-work life that fill you up, that's a problem, too. If your personal-life glass is only half full, you're not going to be in a position to make proactive decisions. So, do anything from go for a run to take a trip somewhere to clear your head a bit. Bowman says, "When we start to achieve professional success, we often leave behind the things that we are truly passionate about." Well, go get them back, lady!

You're Underpaid

In 2023, in both New York State and California, pay transparency laws were passed, making it compulsory to list salaries when advertising positions. According to the New York Department of Labor, "employers with 4 (four) or more employees must include a salary or salary range in their job postings . . . and should give the prospective applicant a legitimate idea of the expected pay."

The idea is to arm prospective employees (you!) with information before you walk into that job interview. In California, from a summary on Cal Matters (calmatters.org), "employers with at least 15 workers will have to include pay ranges in job postings. Employees will also be able to ask for the pay range for their own position. . . ."

And the good news is that you don't need to live in these states for this to be beneficial: it's a fantastic reference tool to get an idea of what you should be paid for a role, wherever you may be based. Knowledge is power!*

Also, you'll obviously find out more through the interviewing process. Lee says, "You might be in a job and go on an interview and find out the job is offering 1.5 times your current salary. Then you're like, 'Oh my gosh, am I being underpaid right now?!' Interviewing can bring awareness to things that you didn't even realize. It can get too comfortable when you're just staying, doing the same thing at the same company for a while."

Gear Up to Go

If you're mentally heading for the door, get some advice, and lots of it. HR and talent expert Bucky Keady recommends that, ideally, you talk to an executive coach as you chart your exit course. "Find one who really goes through all the different steps with you, starting with refreshing your LinkedIn. Also talk to your accountant, financial investment adviser, or lawyer, if you have them." In other words, make sure you're taking a comprehensive approach to your leaving. There's no point in having a perfectly polished résumé if you don't have a few months of savings in the bank to support yourself during your transition. When you voluntarily destabilize

---

* Unfortunately, there aren't pay transparency laws everywhere. For many of our international readers, there will be nothing of the sort in place. There are other ways you can research this more informally though. Try reviewing websites like Glassdoor.com, or even consider reaching out to a few trusted connections in your network to discuss pay expectations within your industry.

your work life, having a financial cushion and an emotional support network will give you confidence to navigate what comes next.

So, what *does* come next? Keady points out, "You can't have the same-old same-old. You have to understand where we are in the workplace. What the opportunities are, where the growth is. Do some serious research on the industries you might be interested in and on what kinds of jobs are open. Then you can reframe yourself."

Retool Your Résumé

Many people overlook how important it is to keep their résumé and LinkedIn profiles current—until they find themselves scrambling to pull it together. Kristina and Laura, having spent most of their careers in long-term roles—a decade-plus here, five years there—hadn't updated a résumé in ages. Don't make the same mistake.

The advantage of deciding to leave your role is that it gives you time to tackle this crucial step.

Lee says, "I think it's very good practice to update your résumé at least once a year, not only to help you keep track of all the great things you've done, but just because you never know what opportunity might come your way."

"It takes a couple of months to pull everything together," says Keady. "Give yourself two to three months to really organize and prepare. Then you've got to practice. What's your stump speech?" Stump speech, elevator pitch, your career for dummies—whatever you want to call it. Have that ready to go . . . when you're ready to go.

Review Your Day-to-Day Budget

If you have an inkling that things are unstable at work, you want to make sure you know what's going on in your bank account. The first step is to "know where your money is going and create a budget," says financial expert Jennifer Barrett. If you need a formula to get you going, try this one: "Fidelity has a good rule of thumb, which is to aim to allocate no more than half of your take-home pay to essential expenses. Save 15 percent of the pre-tax income for retirement savings. Keep 5 percent of your take-home pay for short-term savings, and then use the rest however you'd like."

If the mere idea of a formula melts your brain, at least do some diligence so you're familiar with your financial situation before you walk out the door. Ellevest's senior financial planner Sofia Figueroa says, "Personal finance is called *personal* finance for a reason, and that's because every situation is unique. If someone's harping on you because you spend more than 30 percent of your budget on your housing costs, well, look at what rent prices are. You might be paying more rent if you want to live in a big city, which is giving you other opportunities for your work or your life."

Talk to Others Who Quit Before You Do

A great way to gird your loins is to have conversations with any self-fired friends or acquaintances. People are generally happy to give advice, especially when it makes them look like ballers.

Jessica Goodman, a brilliant YA author who helped us research this book, has a story from her own experience: "Before I quit my job as an editor at *Cosmopolitan* to focus more on writing novels and editorial freelancing, I spent nearly a year thinking about the decision and a couple of months reaching out to every single person I knew who had done something similar—former colleagues who had gone freelance, author friends who had given up their full-time jobs, etc. I asked them all to hop on the phone or if I could take them out to breakfast and peppered them with questions about the transition.

"This worked for a few reasons: I learned so much about what kinds of opportunities were out there, what to do (and what not to do). But it also let people know that I would soon be ready for all kinds of work. When I finally did quit, I emailed every single person I had spoken to during that time and told them I was available for work and if they had any leads or projects they didn't have time to accept, I'd love to be in the loop. This led to a bunch of lucrative copywriting gigs, a ghostwriting job, and editorial contracts. On the flip side, I had friends who had the same experience—wanted to quit, called a bunch of folks who did—and then made a different decision based on those conversations."

Goodman continues, "Speaking to folks in your industry who walked away from their positions can really help you understand if it's the right call for you, and if the work you *think* will be there for you will actually be there."

Some Insurance: A Side Hustle

Do you have another professional-ish passion outside your job? Give it some water and help it grow. "If you have the capacity—

and by capacity I mean you have a little bit of savings—use it as an opportunity to think about how you could be more creative in your next role and maybe have more autonomy and ownership in whatever you do next," says financial expert Farnoosh Torabi. "For me, it was a book. I was like, 'OK, you can lay me off from a job. You can't lay me off from my own book.' You can't lay someone off from their Substack or their Instagram feed or their podcast."

Just be prudent about what that side project is, and be sure it isn't in conflict with your soon-to-be-former company. The great thing is, even if you get another job, "You can have your own thing going on in the event of something else happening that you can't control."

You know, like being fired.

Oprah Winfrey

Oprah is a mononymous media brand and owner—television host, producer, actress, and author. She was fired from the co-anchor position at WJZ-TV evening news in Baltimore in 1977.

"The setback is a setup."

What Happened

At nineteen, I was hired as a news anchor in Nashville. At twenty-two, I moved to Baltimore to co-anchor the WJZ-TV evening news. There was this huge campaign for me coming to Baltimore called "What is an Oprah?" My picture was on the back of buses, on billboards. "What is an Oprah?" ran twenty times a day on TV. People in the commercial were saying, "Do you mean *okra*? Do you mean *opera*? What is an *Oprah*?"

When I started on the local evening news, I was basically in the same situation as Barbara Walters when she went national with Harry Reasoner [in 1976] and whom he treated like dirt under his shoe. My co-anchor was a guy named Jerry Turner. He was white-haired, older, a Ted Baxter from *The Mary Tyler Moore Show*–looking guy. When I arrived, he was condescending, insulting, and rude to me all the time behind the scenes. And I would just take it, because that's what we did in those days; ha ha, laugh it off.

I began my job in the fall of '76 and by the next April Fools' Day, I got called into the general manager's office. He goes, "Sit down. Would you like a ginger ale? Oh, and we're no longer going to have you on the six o'clock news." I said, "Oh, so I'm just going to do the eleven?" "No, you're not going to do the eleven either. You're going to be on your own spot in the 7:25 a.m. cut-in."

I said to him, "Is this an April Fools' joke?" And he said, "You're so good. You should be by yourself on the 7:25 a.m. cut-in (networks usually take a break in their morning programming to cut to their local stations for weather and all that stuff). We're going to give you your own space." I was like, "So, you're firing me?" He said, "Oh, no, no, no, no, we're not firing you. You're still going to be working for us."

I was dumbfounded. I did everything not to cry. I said, "Why is this happening?"

"Because we just believe that you should be on your own and we're going to put Jerry with Al Sanders."

It felt like the demotion of my life. I could start crying right now. I really have never talked about it.

I thought, "How am I going to survive this in the newsroom? Because *everybody* will know." I felt that it would have been better if I'd been kicked completely out. Now we know differently, but back then it was the shame, the walk of shame with your colleagues, where they *all know*.

Gayle King and I had just become friends; she was a production assistant at the station. [After I was fired] I walked down from the GM's [general manager's] office and I was numb. I still had to do the six o'clock news that night. I said to Gayle, who's sitting at her desk, typing copy, "Meet me in the bathroom *now*!" I go into the bathroom and I break down to her: "I just got fired." She's like, "What? How? Why?"

So, that night I have to sit there with Jerry, who's been rude and condescending to me, and he says, "Oh, babe, I just heard." *Babe.* "I'm so sorry. Oh, that's too bad, babe." Now I know that he had everything to do with it—he'd been going behind my back saying, "I can't work with her. She's too young." Blah, blah.

I had a contract for $22,000 a year, and the next year I was supposed to make $25,000. They didn't want to fire me completely as they would have had to pay out the contract. So, I essentially was demoted to the 7:25 cut-ins and demoted to general assignment reporter. This means you're out covering the centenarian birthdays; I remember doing a piece on a new parrot being born at the zoo. There's a four-alarm fire? I'm with the guy in the truck. "Street reporters" are what they were called.

My first concern was reputational, because I had been on this trajectory: first anchor at nineteen, first Black female anchor in Nashville, there was a whole campaign for me. So, it felt like I wasn't only letting myself down, I was letting other women down. I was letting the *race* down. It's very much like a lot of my girls from South Africa who come to the United States [through the Oprah

Winfrey Leadership Academy for Girls], or foreign students who are carrying the burden of the village they come from. You gotta go back and you gotta make good for your village, and the whole community sends you off. Because my father worked in a barber shop, everybody knew that I was the anchorperson. I'd been the anchorperson in Nashville, and it was a big deal for me to move to Baltimore.

Having to go home and tell my father about what had happened was the hardest thing. I had so much shame. He said, "It's OK. It's happened to all of us. Remember the time I was working as a janitor at Vanderbilt and I got fired?" It was his overnight third job and he had fallen asleep. When he came home and told my stepmother and I that he'd gotten fired, I cried because I thought, "How embarrassing. We're not going to be able to eat, what a shame." He said, "It's going to be OK, I'll find another job." And he said the same thing to me: "You're going to be fine."

But I do think it's the only time in my career, the only time in my life, that I felt that something I had done was not good enough, and therefore, *I* wasn't good enough. The only time I actually felt like, well, I failed. I did the best I could, and it still wasn't good enough. I failed. The embarrassment and shame of that was hard to bear.

Sticking It Out

I was so humiliated by that guy, Jerry. I remember once we were testing the look of a new set. He and the weather guy started asking me, "What school did you go to?" I said, "I went to Tennessee State University."

"Oh, is that a real school, what is that? Is that like a two-year college or what is that?" I said, "It's a four-year college, a Historically Black College."

"Oh, OK. Never heard of it." And then he was saying, "So, weren't you born in Mississippi, is that not by the Mississippi River?" I said, "No. I never saw a river."

"Well, you know about the Mississippi River, don't you? Are you on a tributary of the Mississippi River?" I said, "Well, you know, I was five or six years old when I left, so . . ." They started quizzing me about where the Mississippi River began and where all the tributaries were. At the time, I just felt badly. Like, "Oh God, I gave the wrong answer."

One time, I was told by the news director that I had to cut my hair because it was affecting the chroma key in the background. The assistant news director came to me and said, "Your hair is too wide, and we have to do something about that." I said, "OK, I'll see if I can get a new hairdo."

"No, there's someplace we want to send you to see if they can fix that for you." That's how I ended up bald. They also said, "Your eyes are also a little far apart and your nose is too wide, and your lips are too big. Are you willing to do something about that?" I can hear it in my ear now. And I said, "I don't know. What would I do?" He said, "Well, have you ever considered plastic surgery?" and I said, "No, I would never let somebody cut on my face."

What's interesting is it never occurred to me that it was racist. I thought I just wasn't pretty enough. I thought if I were prettier, he wouldn't have said that to me. So, it's a big revelation for me, even this late in life. I just had the forbearance that I never believed

I was anywhere where I didn't deserve to be. I never had impostor syndrome.

I never believed that "Oh, I've been given this job because I'm Black or because I'm a woman." I realized that I brought value to whatever I was doing. That's why I felt such shame in being fired from the six o'clock news. Had I felt like I was an impostor from the beginning, it would have been a whole different story. It never occurred to me. Now I look back on lots of things that happened and I think that was really misogyny, or that was racism. But at the time it happened, I thought, "If I were prettier, he wouldn't have said that. They think I'm not pretty enough."

What Next

I got through my months of street reporting for WJZ-TV but couldn't wait to leave. I tried to get a job at KYW in Philadelphia. I applied to WCCO in Minneapolis because that's where Mary Tyler Moore had thrown her hat. A destination! I tried for other jobs but no one would hire me. And then a year later, in 1978, I got called up to another general manager at the station. He said, "We're going to start a talk show. Would you be interested in doing this local morning talk show?" I don't know if it was foresight, or they just didn't want to pay out the contract.

The show was called *People Are Talking*. And that's when my life changed. The moment I sat on the talk show—interviewing the Carvel ice cream man and his multiple flavors, and Benny from *All My Children*—the moment I started talking, something felt like I had entered the home space for myself. I knew instantly, "Oh, *this* is what I should be doing."

What that taught me, and has forever been a life lesson, is that life closes a door and it gives room and space for a new door to flourish. And an open window to be offered to you. Had that not happened, I would have continued to be dutiful, to be loyal, because even at twenty-two, I remember my father saying to me, "Twenty-two thousand dollars and you're twenty-two? You're not gonna make that kind of money."

I was never happy being a reporter or being an anchorperson, because I would always get written up as a reporter for being too emotional. I would get notices from my news director: "We heard you went back and gave the family blankets; you can't do that."

"Well, they were burned out of their home, so I got all these blankets and I took them blankets." Another family: "Well, they lost everything, I took them Christmas shopping." Again: *"You can't do that!"*

I was always trying to stifle myself. That's why every time the red light would come on, I'd go into my Barbara Walters position and my Barbara Walters voice and I don't know where that voice came from. When I look at myself on tape now, I go, "Who's that?"

When It Clicked In

I had a really clarifying moment when I was hosting the talk show. I didn't do anything at the time, but I was holding the secret of my own sexual abuse. I never told anyone; nobody knew that I had been sexually assaulted at nine. Literally, raped at nine and then sexually assaulted up until fourteen. Nobody knew. And on this talk show, a young Black woman appeared one day, shortly after I started, and told a story of her sexual molestation by an uncle. I had never heard anyone else share that story. I was in tears, and I could not speak. Afterward, I went to the greenroom to see her. I shut the door and said, "Oh my God, I'd never heard a story like that before. Other than myself. You just told my story." She said, "Why didn't you say something?" And I said, "I was too embarrassed. I was ashamed. But you have now given me the courage to do it." It crystallized then that the ability to use a show as a platform for sharing stories was what I was meant to do. You can use it instead of allowing it to use you.

[Winfrey then moved to Chicago to host *AM Chicago*, which was subsequently named *The Oprah Winfrey Show*.] After I was hired in Chicago, WJZ-TV, the station that wanted me off the air, decided they weren't going to let me out of my contract to go to Chicago [because *People Are Talking* was a success]. Chicago said, "We will wait for you." They waited another six months for me to get out of that contract in Baltimore. And before I came, they wanted to talk about what the promotion was going to be. I said, having learned the lesson from the buses and blah, blah, blah, I want no campaign. I want nothing. I want to just come on the air and let word of mouth do it. And that's exactly what happened.

The show premiered on New Year's Day 1984, and I went out

into the street afterward. People were saying, "Hey, you're that girl on the show!" By the next month, everybody was just calling it "The Oprah Show." Later that year, we changed the name to *The Oprah Winfrey Show*.

I wasn't in a position to put that many protections around myself. I think I was making $100,000 at the time that I left Baltimore, [and it went up] to $235,000. I thought, "That's it, I'm hiring a decorator! That's it forever!" I had a pretty strong deal, like $235, 250, 275, 300,000 and then what happened was *The Color Purple* came along. Because the film required me to be on set for at least two months and I only had two weeks of vacation, I agreed to give up every vacation for the next five years if they would let me film *The Color Purple*. That's how much it meant to me. So, in the process of doing that, I said, I won't take a raise.

The *Oprah* show became so popular, so successful. My attorney at the time said there should be another big negotiation because "What you have is so much more than anybody expected. You should own yourself because you never again want to be in a position where you give up yourself to do what you want to do. You want to be in partnership with people where you can design your own time around what's important for you." That was the life-changing deal: that's when Harpo [Winfrey's production company] was born.

We had all the control. And I had a percentage: I started out with like 35 percent and ended up in the end, I think, with 92 percent. Everything changed with ownership because then I made my own decisions. There was no show that had to go through the corporate sieve of what you could or could not do. I produce it, I give it to you, and you don't get to tell me what it is I do. It was the best thing that ever happened. You can be as authentic as you need to be when you have all the authority. When you carry the authority for yourself.

What I Learned

What I know for sure is that everything is in order. As bad as you feel on the day you're fired, the bounce-back is equally as spectacular. There is no measurement for how bad I felt. I felt shame, I felt disgrace, I felt embarrassment. But I didn't feel suicidal. I didn't feel like, "Oh, my life is over." I felt humiliated. I felt all of those things . . . *but* the satisfaction and the sense of jubilation and joy I felt the moment I sat down at the talk show, I knew I'd found my home. I'd come home to myself. I also realized, that's why all of that happened: to get me here.

What I would say to my younger, fired self is, "Hold on. It's coming. It and all its glory is coming. This is just a closed door leading you to the next level that you couldn't see for yourself." I'd felt blind loyalty to that position. You're an anchorwoman and everybody thinks that's such a big deal even though you don't feel it yourself.

One of the reasons I was able to let go of the greatest position in the world for me [Winfrey ended *The Oprah Winfrey Show* in 2011] was because I was able to separate the show from myself. The platform of the show and all it brought me—financial wealth, influence, attention—I was letting go of *that*. But I would be the same.

For women who identify with their jobs to the point that you think that you *are* your job—take time to separate *you* from the thing that you do. I am Oprah, with all of my values and essences that really matter to me, that make me human, that make me whole, that make me kind and make me generous. That also, you know, make me sad and feel sometimes taken advantage of or not as appreciated. All those things that make me *me* remain intact, even when the show is gone.

Sometime in 1989, I started this principle of intention that we worked from with the staff. If we are not clear about what the intention is, then we don't do it. The intention is going to determine what comes back. So, I had everyone trained in this philosophy of "What is it you really intend?" Before I would go into an interview with anybody, I would ask, "Tell me what you intend. What do you want to happen at the end of this interview? Because I'm the one that can make that happen. And now let me tell you what *I* want to happen at the end of this interview." Being able to do that really changed the trajectory of the show. It makes a more forceful interview; everybody is in alignment.

And so, my intention when I was sitting there was to be in absolute truth with myself. I never wanted to fake it; not for a cookie, not for a recipe, not for nothing. And it got to the point where on a show I could hear myself saying, "Oh my God, what mascara did you use for that makeover? I can't even *believe* your hair!" I could hear myself not being true to myself. It wasn't fresh and it didn't feel authentic. Coming up with ideas that allowed me to grow became harder and harder. I mean, literally, somebody once came in and said, "What if we work with Virgin and we take someone out into space, and we film that?"

I didn't want to reach the point where I'd be stretching out of myself. To be somebody that I'm not, because everybody who's grown up with me and watched all these years would know it. And if it cannot be true, it's time to let it go. And that's what I did. I essentially fired myself.

I know you energetically bring to yourself exactly what you need to move forward. It may look like a setback, and it certainly feels like a setback. But this setback is really a setup for the future. Whatever is going on with you—emotionally, spiritually, energetically—has come into your life to teach you something really profound about yourself. And it showed up to show you a better way forward for yourself. That is always the case. The setback is a setup. You've set me free to find the thing I really should be doing.

That's the perspective that you should look at it from: This just happened to me. It feels bad. It feels like rejection because it *is* rejection. I've been rejected by this to be openly received and embraced by what the next level, the forces of life, have in store for me.

I say this particularly when you've lost somebody in your life and you're grieving. I've learned about grief through the twenty-one dogs that have all been members of my family. Each one passing has taught me something new about life and death: you lose the physical body, but the energy of the spirit remains and abides. And if you open yourself to that which remains, your life gets sweeter. Open yourself to what comes from the rejection and momentary embarrassment of being let go, and the life adventure, the experiences, the encounters, the lessons just get sweeter.

So, I would say don't marinate in the shame of it. Allow yourself to be open to the exaltation that's going to come from it. You shall be exalted.

23

Onward!

Cool Girls Reinvent Themselves

Remember when you were in that sandpit? That stuck time before your stunning metamorphosis? Seems like another lifetime now that you're on this endless beach, doesn't it? Wherever you have landed, congratulate yourself on getting there. What seemed insurmountable is now nothing but a little speed bump on the way to your professional autobahn. The future that you thought was taken from you is now *owned* by you.

What you've experienced, hopefully, is a Capital *R* Revelation: you have options you never knew you had, in worlds you'd never explored, working with people you really respect. And hopefully, after reading the previous chapters, you are not only inspired, you are *prepared*.

A year or two down the post-fired road, you'll be amazed at

where you find yourself. (It's kind of like a breakup: it *sucked* at the time, but now you can't even remember their name.) If you own that you got fired and unpack that shame that so many women voluntarily place on themselves, you will own your future.

Turns out, so many of you already know that, even if it took you a minute to get there. While we were planning this book, we provided a contact email and asked women to share their firing experiences with us (again, that's the whole idea: more sharing, less shame!).

We were privileged to have so many women do just that (some of whom had never told their real story to anyone). To all of you ladies, thank you from the bottom of our hearts for your openness, your trust in us, and, most importantly, your hard-earned wisdom. Here, some learnings:

Cool Girls Who Had Epiphanies

"It was a terrible thing. And then, it became a beautiful thing. I've entered an accidental new journey in my forties that is awakening me to a newness—ways of seeing the world and myself—that I would never have been open to if not for getting fired."

—*Carrie Ko, SVP, Product Management, SMB Growth*

"With each firing, did I ever tell people it was my decision to leave either job? No. Why? Because I had nothing to be ashamed of. Just because I wasn't the right fit for them (or there wasn't a budget) doesn't mean *I* don't fit. It doesn't take away from my talents and contributions. Also, there is power in telling the truth. Am I always this positive and have this self-belief? No. Do I sometimes feel useless and lost? Yes. Do I give myself a good talking-to and move forward? Yes! Because I deserve it. I am thrilled to see more women talking about this and changing the culture around being fired. As cliché as it might sound, it is just the beginning. It's the time to take hold of the reins and go wherever you want!"

—Sarina Bellissimo, Broadcaster

"Just realizing you're not alone is so impactful when you're trying to figure out who you are and what comes next in your career journey (and in that process, learning that your job isn't everything!)."

—Sarah Creelman, Regional Communications Lead—Asia

"I still hold grief for the jobs I've lost and those 'close but no cigars,' and I think that grief is present for a lot of people. I hope your book will touch on how 'all the cool girls have stopped trying to squash down complex feelings and just coexist with them even if it's uncomfy.'"

[We hope we did, Steph!]
—Stephanie Nero, Editor and Content Strategist

"I am reflecting and resetting. Lots of tears and plenty of fear. For the first time in thirty years, I am taking the time to look at my values, where I derive my self-esteem from, and the realization that as much as I am a champion of being brilliant, extroverted, a connector, and warrior on the outside—inside needs to come first."

—Melissa Hopkins,
Senior Strategy, Media, and Marketing Executive

"I'm back to searching for a job again, but that break was needed and I think it's important for all of us to reflect and give ourselves that grace. It's the new normal. We all served our roles with distinction and will go on to do equally great things."

—*Johanna Fuentes, former Head of Global Communications and Public Affairs at Warner Bros.*

"I questioned myself a lot. What was I doing, what did I want, should I move, had I failed, what do I do next? I felt some shame. It took me a while to build myself back up . . . I have never spoken about it to anyone, feeling protective of myself and my reputation. However, the older I get, the more experiences I share, the more conversations I have with intergenerational women, the more I hope insight, stories, and adventure will inspire and connect others."

—*Carrie Mitchell, former Head of Communications at BBH USA*

"The feelings of fear, inadequacy, anger, and heartbreak were debilitating and led to me taking a hard look at my ties between work and worth. It has taken me years to untangle them, and the struggle to keep the two separate still catches up to me sometimes. Like many hard knocks, I can look back and feel lucky that it kicked off me shaping my own career—which I may have never opted for myself."

—*Jacqueline Cooke Lawson, Founder of nursery design studio Mersene Studios*

"I realized that all my life, I've wanted to be like a rock—solid, steadfast, and unyielding. But now, I see the wisdom in being more like a river. Rivers adapt, find new paths, shape their surroundings, and continue to flow no matter what obstacles they face. As a rock, I never allowed myself to fail, to disappoint, or to not meet expectations. Today, I embrace being like a river. This new perspective is not just about survival; it's about embracing change and flowing with the currents of life and career with resilience and grace."

—*Marta Pichlak-Miarka, Managing Director, OMD*

"I keep going and would love to be part of a community who understands how this whole experience feels."

—*Lesa Hannah, former Beauty Director, ELLE Canada*

"We need to invest in ourselves so that we can do the work we care so much about better than we could if we put ourselves last. Jobs come and go, but what we bring to the table only gets better."

—*Erin Bradley, Nonprofit Communications Director*

"The night I was fired from my job running the entertainment channel at AOL, the guy I was dating told me he couldn't have sex with me because, "I'm sorry, but you feel like damaged goods to me right now." I tried to laugh, but of course it stung. Anyhow, the next morning while we were having coffee, I got three different job offers. "Damaged goods," I said to him. "No sex for you for a while, honey."

—*Pavia Rosati,*
Founder of travel website and consultancy Fathom

Cool Girls Who Were Rehired

"Found a new job and moved on and this week walked back into the radio station for the first time to do an interview about my next job as CEO of the city's community foundation . . . It was very hard, I learned a lot, and despite going through fire, it was a triumph for me in the end."

—*Genevieve Jacobs, CEO of Hands Across Canberra*

"Fighting every day for a job that I had no chance of keeping was traumatizing. You helped me realize that I might not be as alone as I thought I was and reiterated what I now know to be true—sometimes these setbacks can lead us to better opportunities. I'm thrilled to share that I immediately found a new position at a company that truly values me and my contributions, where I've been able to flourish and grow for the past four years."

—*Melissa Alexander, Retail Real Estate*

Cool Girls Who Went Out on Their Own

"I decided to build my jewelry business full-time. I had gone full circle. After swearing I would Never Work in Fashion Ever Again, I had landed there, but on my own terms, building my own empire. Would I have gotten to where I am if it wasn't for The Devil [boss]? Dunno. But that experience with her was formative, and as irony would have it, I have a damn successful business and I think she'd actually love my pieces."

—*Alex Tempany, Founder of Tempany*

"I'm proud to say two baby firings and one big one and I've never been happier... The last firing catapulted me into one of the most successful IPOs in retail history, with skin in the game (for once). After all those years of creating so much value for the big guys, it was a wonderful feeling to finally be financially rewarded!"

—*Lisa Pomerantz, Brand Consultant*

"Landing flat on my ass professionally sent me into a personal tailspin, one that forced me to parse my professional identity from my personal one. My entire self-worth was wrapped up in my job, which landed me at an all-time low in the self-esteem department... Today, working for myself, I earn five times what I did in that original job. I'm in a happy relationship with a great man, making a living doing what I love."

—*Jess Graves, Founder and Editor of* The Love List

"I was let go from Victoria's Secret after three-plus decades. It took me a few years to heal and find myself, as my identity was tied to the brand (and my position as VP photography). I created my own jewelry business and then moved into coaching. My passion is to help women reclaim their voice and stand in their own power. Because I've done the work, I can help others accelerate their journey."

—*Niki Baratta, Self-Discovery Life Coach*

"It sounds like a cliché, but that terrible boss really did me the biggest favor. I could have done without having my confidence completely crushed, but it also makes the affirmations and wins I achieve through my business feel that much more real. I think it's made me a better boss, too."

—*Jana Stacevic, Designer*

"It's a well-worn narrative that all great beginnings start at an ending, and that's true for us, too. Nonetheless, it didn't feel that way in the beginning (or the end, however you want to see it). At that moment it felt paralyzing, surreal, and scary—if not a teeny, tiny bit hopeful, too.

"Still, we all felt a certain sense of betrayal, of grief, even embarrassment. It stung like a public humiliation handled in the most impersonal of ways. We had just come through a pandemic as a team and started a much-awaited return to the office, joyful at the thought of once again sitting together in a room. Then, in what felt like the world's biggest 'you can't sit with us' moment, we were out—without even a moment to gather our things and say goodbye.

"In our conversations, we learned that every single one of us had dreamed of starting our own businesses, but the fear had always stopped us. The four of us, without knowing, had always wanted to move beyond the parameters of a traditional company, to stop working for someone else's dream, for someone else's benefit.

"In the process, we have discovered untapped talents. The Sunday Scaries are a thing of the past, we work from anywhere with Wi-Fi, the pride we feel in our work is ours to keep.

"There is part of us that wants to say that on that day of The Call we never would have predicted this, but that's actually not

reality. That hope we felt that day reflects what we knew to be true: we are meant for this. Let us be a lesson. In those moments of catastrophic fear, of self-doubt, of hurt—sit in your stillness and find that teeny, tiny bit of hope. It is there. It is whispering to you, and it is telling you with everything it's got: 'YES, YOU SHOULD.'"
—*Kristine Scichilone, Danielle Neumann, Julie Greenberg, and Nicole Kenneally, Co-Founders, OOO-Marketing*

24

Cut to... A Year Since We Started Writing This Book

It has been almost three years since Laura was laid off from *In-Style*, and nearly two since Kristina bit the dust at *WSJ*. Those two fateful days now feel like a world away—the daily routines we were so deeply immersed in like relics of the *Titanic*.

Laura has spent her time building LB Media's business and traveling to new places, grateful for her ability to work from anywhere. She is also deep into her work with (RED), using her fashion and cultural skill set to address the injustices that allow AIDS and other global pandemics to proliferate. She's excited to spend more time in Africa, learning more about the fashion community on the continent and connecting it with the international stage.

Leaving behind the insular space of magazines, Laura's world has grown infinitely bigger. Moving from Sydney to New York once seemed like the biggest leap she could make, but now that seems like hopscotch compared to the long jump. She also manages her time and her energy better, choosing projects carefully and prioritizing friends and family. She walks in Central Park or, when she's home in Australia, like a tourist across the Sydney Harbour Bridge. And she's done with spending time with people, and on things, that don't matter.

Oh, and as for how she felt on those freshly fired days when she was bummed that she wasn't going to Paris for the fashion shows? She kinda forgets when they're on (until Chanel or Balenciaga pop up on Instagram) and sees her designer friends when they're not chained to the studio.

For Kristina, some days it still stings. But here's the thing: getting fired wasn't the end. It was the beginning of something unexpected and, dare she say it, wonderful. The opportunities that have presented themselves over the past two years? Just *wow*. A casual business acquaintance became her boss (hi, Charlie), she joined the Toteme board, and . . . hello, this book!

And then there's the life she's built outside of work. She's more present for her kids and her partner—not in a woo-woo way, but in a grounded, real way. She makes time to read and do Pilates. The cozy moments at home, the deeper conversations, the sense of balance—she wouldn't trade any of it. Getting fired sucked, but sometimes you have to lose the job to find the life.

What has been most edifying is the army of women who have approached us since we announced the book, asking when it would be out, how they can show support, and confirming just how much it's needed. It fills our hearts right up.

And we'll soon be taking a big swing: we are beginning to build out a Cool Girl network, a professional community for women who have either read this book, heard about it—or just gotten fired and have no idea who the hell we are. Bookmark allthecoolgirlsgetfired.com and follow @allthecoolgirlsgetfired on Instagram and TikTok to stay updated.

Our master plan at ATCG is to help you navigate your transition with a wealth of knowledge and a community of supportive voices, ensuring that you can find guidance and encouragement when you need it most. We promise that for every "You go, girl," you will also have a big old laugh. Why? Because you earned it.

We wrote a silly fake blurb when we were brainstorming the book:

"After reading this book, we want to get fired."

—*Everyone*

While it makes us chuckle, the kernel of it is important: life is short. Whether you leave an unfulfilling job or are dumped right out of it, remember that you have regained the most important thing: your independence.

Now take some time to sit on that beautiful beach you'd barely noticed, and *lean out*.

Acknowledgments

First things first: Thank you to the internet. Specifically, the overwhelming wave of women who responded to Laura's "All the Cool Girls Get Fired" Instagram post—starring Laura and Kristina and many wine bottles—in April 2023, which started us on this wildly edifying ride. If it weren't for you ladies, Kristina would never have called Laura the next morning and said, "I think there's a book in this."

To our families, for your patience and love as we navigated the thrilling but dense process of writing this book—from interviewing Carol Burnett to zombie-reading the IRS website. To Kristina's partner, Magnus, for his calm and clarity (and for our book cover!), and her children, Stella and Dexter, for not making it weird when she showed up at school pickup for the first time in years. To Laura's husband, Brandon, for nodding along when she sat on the couch for six hours at a time, pounding out a chapter while loudly announcing, "I'm writing a book!" And to their cat, Batty, for nothing.

To both home teams, for enduring countless hours of the *Jazz for Kittens* playlist (shout-out to Spotify), and for making us laugh—or making us go on a walk—right when we needed it.

To Kay and Larry Richards, Kristina's devoted and tireless parents; her wise-owl brother, Brian, and his no-BS wife, Catherine;

and their awesome kids. (We banged out our book proposal at the Richards' house over Memorial Day weekend 2023 while inhaling margaritas at Larry's seventieth birthday party.) And to Catherine's father, James Breen, who served as our legal-eagle eyes.

To Lola Maddalena, Laura's mom, who said in her concise way, "That's good," when Laura updated her on the book process, and "That's very good," when told that Oprah was in it.

To our brilliant literary agent, Alyssa Reuben, and her team at WME, for believing in this idea and helping us shape the pitch into something tangible, heartfelt, and helpful.

To our sage editor at Gallery Books, Pamela Cannon: we were immediately desperate to please you. Our gratitude for your keen insights, patience, encouragement—and love of a ba-dum ching joke.

To the "Gallery Girls," a.k.a. the incredible broads on the Gallery Books team: Aimée Bell, Sally Marvin, Lauren Carr, Emma Skeels, Hanna Preston, Lisa Litwack, and publisher Jennifer Bergstrom. We knew immediately that we had to go with you (and not just because some of you have been fired and are therefore cool). Your taste, savviness, and humor have been our GPS.

To Andy McNicol, our Book Boss, for helping us usher this book into the world and "Johnny Appleseeding" what's next—we can't wait to turn our ATCG community into a brand.

To Laura's all-powerful unscripted agent, Bradley Singer, and mega-manager, Jason Weinberg, for seeing beyond the book into the realms of screens big and small.

To young legend Alli Armstrong, for keeping the trains on time, even if they were on PST.

To the genius YA author Jess Goodman, who by some miracle found the time to report, research, and interview experts for our service chapters. Your dedication and zing (even when writing about COBRA) made this book so much better.

To the women who are the literal spine of this book: Dominique Browning, Mika Brzezinski, Tarana Burke, Carol Burnett (!!), Lindsay Colas, Katie Couric, Jamie Lee Curtis, Sallie Krawcheck, Lisa Kudrow, Angela Missoni, Margherita Maccapani Missoni, Jennifer O'Connell, Rebecca Quinn, Tracy Sherrod, and, hell yeah, Oprah Winfrey. Thank you for your unbelievable generosity and clarity in sharing such a vulnerable time in your careers. Your strength and candor will immeasurably help anyone who needs it.

To our industry experts, who shared their expertise on everything from finance to "eff it": Jennifer Barrett, Natasha Bowman, Caitlin Donovan, Sofia Figueroa, Catherine Fisher, Phoebe Gavin, Andy Hamilton, Kristy Hurt, Bucky Keady, Lorraine K. Lee, Shannon Liss-Riordan, Jennifer Liu, Sylvia Long-Tolbert, Ron Lieber, Sarah Michalczuk, Jill Mizrachy, Katherine Morgan Schafler, Marianne Ruggiero, Elizabeth Saylor, Farnoosh Torabi, and Ashley Tanks. Your wisdom is a salve.

To the incredible women who emailed us with their stories: you are the heart and soul of this book. Your bravery, humor, and honesty made us emo. We hope we have done you justice. Or at least made you feel cool.

To the friends, mentors, and colleagues who supported us along the way: you kept us going (even the ones who asked, "Do you really want to be the poster girls for getting fired?"). Uh, yes, actually.

Our pals thank-yous are tricky because we have a lot of overlap, so know that, in whatever paragraph you land, you are loved.

Special shout-out from Kristina to Derek Blasberg, Nick Brown, Tory Burch, Julie Coe, Nicole Fritton, Diane von Furstenberg, Thomas Gebremedhin, Rebecca Gradinger, Amy Griffin, Poppy Harlow, Gareth Jones, Elin Kling, Karlie Kloss, Chris Knutsen (appreciate your early read and invaluable feedback), Karl Lindman, Elisa Lipsky-Karasz, J. J. Martin, Natalie Massenet, Rebekah McCabe, Sara Moonves, Matt Murray, Samira Nasr, Andrea Oliveri, Jennifer Pastore, Jamie Patricof, Frances Pennington, Rory Satran, Kelly Sawyer Patricof, Lauren Santo Domingo, Jessica Seinfeld, Johanna Sjöberg, Karina Sokolovsky, Charles F. Stewart, and Dasha Zhukova Niarchos.

Laura's immense appreciation for the friends and co-conspirators who shared ideas, connections, and posts about our book from the minute we signed the deal. Wren Arthur, Renée Beaumont, Bono (for your hot take on the C-Suite), Rose Byrne, Libby Callaway, Malcolm Carfrae, Sali Christeson, Laura Dern, Tom Freston ("That's cool, baby"), Sarah Harden ("FiredFest" is inspired), Kerry Diamond, Iman, Anthony Kendal, Monica Lewinsky (who wrote the funniest possible comment on our first Insta), John Melick, Maggie Morris, Bruna Papandrea, Cindy Palusamy, Michelle Pfeiffer, Christy Turlington Burns, Kiane von Mueffling, Naomi Watts, and John Wattiker.

To Marie-Louise Scio and Dona Daher for your generosity in hosting us at the first-ever "Writer's Room" at Il Pellicano to finish the book. You validated and supported our nascent "authorship," and, as importantly, two pastas (at least) each a day supplied vital carbs to finish the "marathon."

To Glenda Bailey, who brought us together under the mad roof of *Harper's Bazaar*. GB, you'll be delighted there's a flame on our cover.

To Cass Bird, our fantasy photographer, who made us look, well, fire. To the ladies (and gent) who "polished" us for the shoot: Jenna Lyons, Romy Solemani, Jodie Boland, Richie LaPaglia, and Esther Langham—our retoucher also thanks you.

And finally, to DotDash Meredith's Neil Vogel and the *Wall Street Journal*'s Emma Tucker. The door didn't hit us on the way out; it opened even wider.

Stay cool,

LB & KO

About the Authors

LAURA BROWN is the founder of LB Media and the chair of (RED)'s Creative Council. She sits on the boards of (RED); Fashion Trust U.S.; me too. Movement; and Foot Soldiers Park—Selma, Alabama. Previously, she was editor in chief of *InStyle*, executive editor of *Harper's Bazaar*, and senior editor at *W*. She earned a BA in arts and communication from Charles Sturt University in New South Wales, Australia. Brown lives in Manhattan with her husband.

KRISTINA O'NEILL is the head of Sotheby's Media and editor in chief of *Sotheby's Magazine*. Previously, she was editor in chief of *WSJ. Magazine*, executive editor at *Harper's Bazaar*, and held earlier editorial roles at *New York* magazine and *Time Out New York*. She sits on the board of Swedish fashion brand Toteme and is a Citymeals on Wheels ambassador. A graduate of NYU's Gallatin School of Individualized Study, she serves on the school's Alumni Council. O'Neill lives in Brooklyn with her family.